Comments on other *Amazing Stories* from readers & reviewers

"You might call them the non-fiction response to Harlequin romances: easy to consume and potentially addictive."
Robert Martin, *The Chronicle Herald*

"Tightly written volumes filled with lots of wit and humour about famous and infamous Canadians."
Eric Shackleton, *The Globe and Mail*

"This is popular history as it should be ... For this price, buy two and give one to a friend."
Terry Cook, a reader from Ottawa, on **Rebel Women**

"Stories are rich in description, and bristle with a clever, stylish realness."
Mark Weber, *Central Alberta Advisor*, on **Ghost Town Stories II**

"The resulting book is one readers will want to share with all the women in their lives."
Lynn Martel, *Rocky Mountain Outlook*, on **Women Explorers**

"[The books are] long on plot and character and short on the sort of technical analysis that can be dreary for all but the most committed academic."
Robert Martin, *The Chronicle Herald*

"A compelling read. Bertin ... has selected only the most intriguing tales, which she narrates with a wealth of detail."
Joyce Glasner, *New Brunswick Reader*, on **Strange Events**

"The heightened sense of drama and intrigue, combined with a good dose of human interest is what sets Amazing Stories *apart."*
Pamela Klaffke, *Calgary Herald*

REBEL WOMEN
OF THE KLONDIKE

AMAZING STORIES®

REBEL WOMEN OF THE KLONDIKE

Extraordinary Achievements and Daring Adventures

RICH MOLE

For Shirley, the "rebel woman" of my life

PUBLISHED BY ALTITUDE PUBLISHING CANADA LTD.
1500 Railway Avenue, Canmore, Alberta T1W 1P6
www.altitudepublishing.com
www.amazingstories.ca
1-800-957-6888

Extreme care has been taken to ensure that all information presented in
this book is accurate and up to date. Neither the author nor the
publisher can be held responsible for any errors.

Publisher	Stephen Hutchings
Associate Publisher	Kara Turner
Editors	Heather Hudak & Jane Grove
Cover & layout	Zoe Howes

We acknowledge the financial support of the Government
of Canada through the Book Publishing Industry Development
Program (BPIDP) for our publishing activities.

Altitude GreenTree Program
Altitude Publishing will plant twice as many trees as were used
in the manufacturing of this product.

National Library of Canada Cataloguing in Publication Data

A CIP RECORD FOR THIS TITLE IS AVAILABLE UPON REQUEST FROM THE PUBLISHER

Amazing Stories® is a registered trademark of Altitude Publishing Canada Ltd.

For general information on Altitude Publishing and the Amazing Stories, including all books published
by Altitude Publishing, please call our order line at 1-800-957-6888. For reseller information,
including discounts and premium sales, please call our sales department at 403-678-9592.
For press review copies, author interviews, or other publicity information, please contact our
marketing department at 403-283-7934, or via fax at 403-283-7917. For general information,
visit our Web sites: *www.amazingstories.ca* and *www.altitudepublishing.com*

Printed and bound in Canada
2 4 6 8 9 7 5 3 1

Contents

Cast of Characters

Ethel Berry

Annoyed at the thought of having her marriage to a Yukon prospector postponed, Ethel was eager to tie the knot, even if it meant braving the North with her new husband. Within months, fate would decree that she become one of the Klondike's wealthiest women.

Martha (Purdy) Black

For the bored Chicago socialite, wife, and mother, the opportunity to embark on a Klondike adventure was a welcome escape from a mundane routine of upper-class recreational diversions. Life would *never* be boring again.

Nellie Cashman

A teenaged Irish immigrant, Nellie was a veteran of gold camps by the time she was 30. When Klondike gold fever swept the globe, this unorthodox prospector and renowned gold-creek philanthropist embarked on some of her greatest adventures.

Emily Craig

Swept away by gold fever, Emily and her husband decided to enter the Yukon through Edmonton, Alberta. For two agonizing years, Emily endured the horrific hardships of Canada's trail of shame, greed, and deception.

Anna DeGraf

Her husband murdered and her son's whereabouts unknown, seamstress Anna DeGraf might have seemed an impoverished loser. Instead, her personal pluck and selfless assistance to fallen women won DeGraf the admiration of both men and women throughout the Yukon.

Frances Dorley

Chafing under stifling parental control, young Frances left Seattle for a life of northern adventure. Much to her parents' horror, she travelled in the company of men.

Faith Fenton

Renowned Canadian journalist and editor Faith Fenton was down on her luck when the Klondike lured her away from Toronto. The Yukon gold rush gave this single woman an opportunity to report the world's greatest rags-to-riches story.

Nettie Hoven

Desperate to escape a murderous lover, this New Yorker booked passage on a steamer bound for Alaska, surviving shipwreck and cannibalism as she travelled around Cape Horn. She arrived in Dawson City with her obsessed lover in hot pursuit.

Marguerite Laimee

She was a child bride at 14 and a gold-camp adventurer before she was 20. The trail of easy money led this woman of easy virtue to Dawson City. Marguerite did not strike it rich in the mines. Instead, she made her money in matrimony.

Mae McKamish Meadows
Wild West performer Mae and her sharpshooting husband, Charley, had lived a life of make-believe adventure. However, even before they reached the Klondike, the North brought them more real-life adventure than the two performers could handle.

Belinda Mulrooney
Already a businesswoman of note, 24-year-old Belinda focussed her opportunistic energies on the gold creeks and became an entrepreneurial marvel. The Klondike would never be the same.

Kate Rockwell
In the face of personal travail, Kitty's unquenchable spirit catapulted her into the public consciousness as "Klondike Kate" long after the gold dwindled away and left Dawson City little more than a ghost town.

Kate Ryan
Initially, Canadian Kate Ryan began the journey of a lifetime to escape an unrequited love. In the end, it was the lure of the North — and the North-West Mounted Police — that won the heart of this tough-minded, hard-working restaurateur.

Prologue

Mrs. La Ghrist decided she had heard enough. It had been nearly two years since she had laid eyes on her husband, John. Now, after her new beau had paid the lout $1,500 to leave them alone, John La Ghrist was back, begging her to give up her new life in the Klondike and accompany him to Australia. She scoffed. With him? Now? She was doing quite all right, thank you. In Vancouver, on the Stikine Trail, and now in Dawson City, she had always made money from "her girls." If John didn't like it, he could go right back to Hamilton, Ontario, where they had both come from.

Suddenly John demanded something else. He demanded she give him a share of her hard-earned money. She laughed, but when she turned to tell her estranged husband exactly what she thought of him, she was staring down the barrel of his revolver.

People on the street near the alley entrance heard two shots ring out. They turned to see a woman lurch from the open door of a wooden shack, and stagger into the alley. John La Ghrist emerged from the doorway, levelled the revolver at his bleeding wife, and fired again. The woman's body jerked with the bullet's impact. She stumbled in the dust of the alley and began crawling away. Onlookers rushed to her aid as John La Ghrist calmly walked back into the shack and slammed the door. As the stunned bystanders turned over the bleeding, semi-conscious woman, they heard another shot fire inside the shack.

Chapter 1
Compelling Motivations

I n a far-off Alaskan seaport, two steamships slipped their moorings and headed south. On board was a motley collection of passengers who had made the long stern-wheeler journey down the Yukon River to St. Michael, on the Bering Sea.

Less than a year earlier, these individuals had been as impoverished as the poorest unemployed in Chicago, San Francisco, Winnipeg, or Vancouver. Their exhausted demeanour, their gaunt, bearded faces, and the dishevelled, worn clothing that hung on their bodies still gave them the look of the down and out. However, their appearance disguised the fact that, through a combination of luck, timing, and determination, each one of these haggard individuals was now incredibly wealthy. Within days, the personal fortune each had wrested from the frozen ground would bring hope and a sense of purpose to hundreds of thousands of others.

The World They Knew
Historians called the 1890s the Gay Nineties because there was much to be happy about. War was absent from the front pages of the newspapers for the first time in living memory. At last, the civilized world was at peace.

In North America, the anguish of the personal upheaval endured through decades of tumultuous national expansion was a thing of the past. Throughout the continent, the West had been won. In the United States, the Indian Wars were over. In Canada, the Northwest Rebellion had been put down just five years earlier. People were enjoying the benefits of transportation systems and communication innovations that triumphed over time and distance. Railways linked tiny inland outposts with metropolises from coast to coast. Fleets of fast clipper ships were setting records as they brought the New World closer to the Old. Telegraph wires were humming with messages, and soon telephone wires would be buzzing, too.

In urban homes, kitchen taps had replaced iron pumps, flush toilets had replaced outhouses and chamber pots, and electric lights were replacing gas and oil lamps. New, popular music mirrored the bright, lively tempo of the times, as pianos were uncrated and rolled into more and more homes. In well-furnished parlours, the sedate triple metre of a familiar Strauss waltz was often augmented by the strident four-four time of a new Sousa march and the fast-tumbling notes of a Scott Joplin "rag."

In the 1890s, North American society was a comforting blend of two worlds: that of men and that of women. This was nothing new. However, those spheres were about to intersect in ways that the previous generation could not have imagined.

Most women who entered the workplace did so out of dire financial necessity. Women were usually relegated to mind-numbing factory jobs. The more fortunate, employed as nurses and teachers, regarded their professions as temporary positions. They were expected to abandon work as soon as the right man came along, or, certainly, as soon as their first "sickness" (pregnancy) overtook them. Women over 40 years of age who were still emptying bedpans or instructing children were doomed to that most unfortunate of futures — spinsterhood.

Martha (Purdy) Black, who spent most of her adult life in the Yukon, recalled her father's attitude toward women. Her 16-year-old mother bore the brunt of it just minutes after giving birth to Martha and her twin sister.

"Susan, I am disappointed," Martha's father frowned. "I expected a boy."

"Yes, I know," Martha's exhausted mother whimpered. "I am so sorry."

At finishing school, Martha studied subjects typical

for young upper-class women of the time, including elocution and deportment. However, she also successfully mastered "new age" subjects such as calculus and typing. Still, her father's expectations were typical for the times. Upon Martha's graduation, a friend asked her father what career he had selected for the "dear girl." Martha always remembered her father's curt reply.

"The career of a wife and mother," he snapped.

Located in the frozen wilderness of the Far North, the Klondike was, as the *Seattle Post-Intelligencer*'s headline bluntly stated, "No Place For Women."

"Women are utterly unfit to fight the battle out there," one Klondiker concurred, ignoring the fact that most men were also "utterly unfit." That fact didn't stop nearly 30,000 men from setting off from job, home, and family in search of Klondike gold. It was enough to stop most women, though. A woman's place was in the home, not on a gold creek.

* * *

Stay-at-home sentiments were perhaps best expressed by a *London Times* editor, Flora Shaw, who had visited the gold creeks of the Klondike. In a speech she gave to the Royal Colonial Institute in early 1899, Flora told her mostly male audience, "In the expanse of the Empire, as in other movements, man wins the battle, but woman holds the field." The "field" referred to the household.

What Klondike stampeders needed most, the editor told her audience, was what men everywhere needed. Seeming to ignore the possibility that other women might aspire to her own abilities and achievements, Flora thought women should stick to what they did best. Their list of objectives should include: "To clean the spot in which they lived — even if it were only a tent or shack — to wash the clothes, to cook the food, to give to one's fireside a human interest." A charitable observer might conclude that she knew her audience well. However, the separate worlds of men and women seemed to be on a collision course.

For the first time, women were on the march for recognition in the workplace, the ability to own property, and the right to vote. Surely, most right-thinking men told each other, this particular path was not one their own wives and daughters would choose to set foot on. Yet the emancipation movement that had begun so tentatively a decade or two before was to continue more stridently 70 years later.

This, then, was the world that Canadian and American women knew, as they and their families and friends celebrated the start of this final tranquil decade in a century of upheaval and hardship. Women were poised to enjoy a gentler, better, *happier* world than their mothers and grandmothers had ever known.

Just when expectations were at their highest, dark clouds of discontent and despair were gathering on the sunny horizon of the twentieth century.

Desperate Times

On November 11, 1890, Henry Swift, the general manager of Nova Scotia's huge Springhill Mines operation, was worried. The mine conditions were dark and dangerous. Pit boys working for a pittance were forever beset with bruises and broken bones. Workers faced threatening water levels, rotting timbers, and pockets of poison gas. A miner's lot had not changed much in a century.

"I am doing all I can to keep things straight and can do no more," Henry wrote to his boss. It was, he added, "enough worry to kill a man."

Mere worry didn't kill Henry Swift. The day after he wrote that letter, a mine shaft was rocked by a fiery blast. That explosion ended Henry's life, as well as those of 124 other beloved husbands and sons. Canada's worst mining disaster was an ominous portent of things to come.

A little more than a year later, in Homestead, Pennsylvania, disgruntled Carnegie Mill steel workers took off their gloves, dropped their shovels, and walked off the job. Hired enforcers attempted to coerce the men back. Families grieved as eighteen men died in the street fights that followed.

In 1893, shortly after the new year had been rung in, the impossible occurred: the Philadelphia and Reading Railroad went bankrupt. Banks and their mortgage company cousins began to close their doors, shutting out tens of thousands of stunned depositors and lenders. Savings and investments vanished. Before the year staggered to its conclusion, three other major American railroads had parked their locomotives and dismissed thousands of employees.

By this time, one-sixth of the American workforce — four million angry, desperate men and women — were unemployed. Staring into empty wallets, people all over North America simply stopped spending. Scores of retail outlets closed their doors in response.

Economic conditions were bleakest in the Pacific Northwest. Many began to walk exposed sandy beaches at low tide to dig up clams for the kitchen table. Unaccustomed to the humiliation of rejection, the men grew despondent. In turn, wives endured their frustrated husbands' anger and the whining of hungry children. The descendants of one such Washington State family never forgot those tough times.

John and Emma Feero had five children. Family size had always been a source of pride for Feero, so long as his Tacoma transportation company was profitable. Railroad closures hit hard. Feero lost everything but two horses and a wagon. Clamouring to be fed, his large family became a crushing responsibility. As John relentlessly searched for work, Emma scrimped and made do. The family was forced to relocate five times in four years.

A Godsend from the North

In the summer of 1897, two coastal steamers disgorged their precious Klondike cargoes in San Francisco and Seattle. The arrival of the ships triggered the last and greatest gold rush in history.

"Gold! Gold! Gold! Gold!" screamed the headline of the *Seattle Post-Intelligencer* on Saturday, July 17, 1897. In a depressed port city full of desperate people, gold meant the end of hardship and want. Gold was something few people had, nearly everybody dreamed about, and many would do anything to get their hands on. For 68 rich arrivals on the steamship *Portland*, and dozens more who had hefted their bullion off the *Excelsior* in San Francisco two days earlier, that dream had come true. They had found what everybody wanted — bags, boxes, and rawhide bundles of gold — and had brought it back home to tempt the rest of the world. The two ships had brought in two million dollars worth of temptation, the *San Francisco Chronicle* reported. More than a century later, this amount still signifies wealth. At a time when a 50-cent piece bought a full-course dinner at a respectable restaurant, the sum was almost unimaginable.

"Going To Scoop Up The Gold," trumpeted the *San Francisco Call* five days after the *Portland's* headline-making arrival. That day, the overloaded steamer was churning the water of the Puget Sound, on its way back up the coast once again. The decks were crammed; every stateroom was taken. Among the hundreds squeezed on board those first over-booked boats was John Feero. His wife, Emma, had agreed to stay home with the kids while he went north to strike it rich. Happy days were here again.

Nearly one year later, the North-West Mounted Police estimated 19,000 would-be prospectors had passed through customs posts on their journey over the mountains and down the Yukon River to Dawson City. Fewer than 700 of these hopefuls — a meagre 3.5 percent — were women. But in an era when most men did whatever they wanted and many women found they could not, it is astonishing that the gold-hungry hordes included any women at all.

Blissful Ignorance

News of enormous gold discoveries flashed by telegram up the coast and to the east after the *Excelsior* tied up in San Francisco that Thursday. The ship had taken the California port city by surprise. When the *Portland* edged up against the wharf's timbers in Seattle two days later, thousands were waiting on the waterfront, eager to witness the parade of new millionaires staggering down the gangway and heaving their riches aboard waiting wagons. Gold fever was about to hit its zenith, infecting tens of thousands of men — and many women, as well. One of them was Wild West performer Mae McKamish Meadows, who had been living in Santa Cruz, California.

"The people have gold sacked up like wheat lying all around," the excited woman wrote to relatives back home when she and her sharpshooter husband, Charley, hit Juneau, Alaska. Mae hadn't actually seen the gold (she was quoting a letter from faraway Dawson City), but, she enthused, the reports "would make you want to have a flying machine and go at once!" Mae's hopes were high. "If we can only get in we will be ready to come back next summer and buy out Santa Cruz!"

In Chicago, Emily Craig and her husband of 10 years were leading a quiet, comfortable life when the Klondike strikes made headlines. The Craigs were thrilled by the newspaper stories. Not long afterward, her husband confessed to Emily that he had actually seen some Klondike nuggets in a jeweller's store display. The very next day, Emily stood with her nose pressed to the store window, gazing at the gold on the other side of the glass, as enraptured as her husband had been. "From then on, I could believe any story," she admitted. "We both caught gold fever — and that is no childhood disease, either." The Craigs were soon on their way across the country.

Not all women who said goodbye to friends and family to make the trek to the Yukon were naïve. Ethel Berry, who left a full year ahead of the mob with her new husband, Clarence, knew a little of what lay ahead.

"I was prepared for the hardships, having known perfectly well before I decided to go that it would be no bed of roses," Ethel said. Ethel had the advantage of insider information: Clarence had already been prospecting in the Yukon for two years.

In early 1898, New Yorker Marie Riedeselle decided to join the rush. However, before she boarded her ship, the former Connecticut farmer undertook a three-month strategic plan to learn as much as she could about the Klondike. This exercise was so unusual (most *men* did no planning) that Marie's efforts caught the attention of the *Seattle Daily Times.*

Marie "knows accurately the geography of the country, knows the customs and habits of the people there, the kind of garments best adapted to the climate," the newspaper reported. Marie's unseemly behaviour intensified as she actually attempted to master the physical skills she thought she would need, including "how to handle dogs, manage a loaded sled, propel a boat; in fact how to do everything a human being needs to do in that country." These skills took strength and stamina. The former masseuse undertook a daily physical workout with the same zeal as she conducted her research, "and," the reporter assured his bemused readers, "her muscles are in perfect condition for her great undertaking."

Ethel and Marie were exceptions. For most, ignorance was bliss. Why spoil the fun? It was all so easy — just buy a ticket, pack your clothes, and "Ho, for the Klondike!"

"Women have made up their minds to go to the Klondike, so there is no use trying to discourage them ... our wills are strong and courage unfailing," a woman reporter told readers of *The Skagway News.*

Soon, however, hundreds of women would learn that strong wills and unfailing courage would scarcely be enough. Their lessons would come quickly — and painfully.

Chapter 2
Nothing to Lose

F or the "weaker sex" to join the adventure of the gold rush appeared to be folly and madness. The Yukon terrain was so hostile, and living conditions so horrific, that the experience quickly drove the strongest men to acts of madness, and even suicide. Like the men, women of the Klondike often risked everything. What would compel a woman to endure discomfort and danger, including freezing and frostbite, flash flood, fire, and avalanche? Why would a woman risk the ravages of scurvy, tuberculosis, pneumonia, meningitis, and typhoid — diseases that shortened or destroyed the lives of thousands of Klondikers?

For most men, and some women, too, the obvious answer was gold — the chance to strike it rich. For others, the answers were far more complex.

Sensing an Opportunity

Belinda Mulrooney stood in shock and dismay. Across the busy San Francisco street, the firemen had done their best, but it was too little, too late. Belinda watched as the building that housed her newly sublet restaurant continued to smoulder. For weeks, she had poured time, effort, and money into the dilapidated structure. Her new West Coast real estate venture had eaten up most of the $8,000 profit from the sale of her restaurant in the Chicago World's Fair. Now all of that capital had gone up in smoke.

The fire was a disastrous setback for the young woman who had enjoyed a rags-to-riches experience since coming to America as an impoverished Irish teenager. Years before, her parents had fled the Emerald Isle in search of a better life, leaving their little girl behind. When she was just 13, Belinda set sail to join her family in the United States. Reuniting with her estranged family in Archibald, Pennsylvania, was not a happy occasion. Belinda didn't like the coal dust of the Pennsylvania mines, or her family. They were dirt-poor Irish. Within weeks of their ill-fated reunion, Belinda became obsessed with one thought: she must make enough money to leave. Her mother, Maria, was not pleased when Belinda left for the biggest city in the state, Philadelphia. Little wonder. The last time Belinda's mother had laid eyes on her, she was still a toddler.

"You are the queerest human being I ever saw in my life," Maria Mulrooney told her willful daughter. "I don't understand you."

Once in Philadelphia, it wasn't long before Belinda was hired as a nanny by a wealthy couple. It was a dream come true. Unlike Belinda's father, George King Cummings and his wife, Belle, did not awaken at 4 a.m. to crawl — literally *crawl* — down a coal mine.

The Cummings taught Belinda many lessons.

"What's this?" Belinda asked Belle. Her pay cheque, Belle explained. Belinda handed it back. "Save it for me." Belinda had never been in a bank. Belle took her there to establish a savings account.

The teenage nanny began to formulate ideas about life. She thought it would be nice to have a house like the Cummings', to dress the way they dressed, to speak the way they spoke, and to have money. She believed the secret to obtaining these luxuries was to become an entrepreneur.

Soon Belinda was reading newspaper stories about factory shutdowns. Mr. Cummings was worried. Belinda listened carefully when her employer explained about the financial crash. Belinda then offered to lend the family her entire $600 bank account. Times were difficult, Belle Cummings laughed, but not that difficult.

Belinda knew better. She could wait and worry, or take matters into her own hands. After a casual visit with the cook and the housemaid next door, Belinda decided to take action. The women decided to open a restaurant in Chicago, where the 1890s' version of the world's fair, the World's Columbian Exposition, was being built, complete with canals, a lagoon, graceful iron-and-glass buildings, and a new invention called the Ferris wheel. However, it wasn't long before Belinda sensed a new opportunity in California. She sold the restaurant and moved south.

Now, with her San Francisco property a smoking ruin and most of her Chicago fair proceeds gone, Belinda decided to search for job prospects on the waterfront.

"What can you do?" Thomas R. Turner snapped. As Pacific Coast Steamships' port steward, Turner had no time for a young woman looking for a job when so many men were out of work.

"I don't know," Belinda admitted. "Tell me what I have to do and I will do the best I can."

Turner looked at the woman in front of him more closely. She was short but well-built, and she had unflinching, calculating eyes behind steel-rimmed spectacles. "Well, what do you *want* to do?" he asked.

Belinda remembered seeing posters advertising passage to a new and exciting destination. "I want to work on one of the ships going to Alaska."

"Out of the question," Turner replied. "They don't carry stewardesses." Then Turner remembered a note from the *Santa Rosa*, one of two ships on the San Diego run. A stewardess had fallen sick. Turner made Belinda an offer. She accepted.

A few weeks later, Belinda was knocking on Turner's office door again.

"Thanks, Mr. Turner, but I'm looking for something else. Too many whiny women on that run."

Turner couldn't ignore the *Santa Rosa*'s reports describing how hard the feisty little woman had worked.

"Okay, Miss Mulrooney," he replied. Perhaps she would be more comfortable with rough-and-ready men. "I'll try you on the Alaska run."

Three years later, Belinda's desperate flight from poverty would lead her to Dawson City in the Yukon. Again, mining figured prominently in her life, but she wouldn't work on her hands and knees as her father had done. Instead, she would stand tall, as a mine owner and broker who bought and sold others' mines. The girl who had nothing to lose in Pennsylvania found she had everything to gain in the Klondike. Belinda Mulrooney was not alone.

Nellie Cashman had an important decision to make.

Like Belinda Mulrooney, this Irish teenage hopeful had set sail for the United States and a better life. Nellie found it in an unlikely, unladylike setting: a raw, raucous gold camp in 1870s Nevada. The only woman in the place and still unmarried, Nellie somehow retained her virtue and earned the admiration of the men. When not actively prospecting, she ran a boarding house. As gold and silver petered out, Nellie, determined and adventurous, decided to tag along with hundreds of prospectors to British Columbia's remote Cassiar gold fields.

Nellie loved her footloose lifestyle and followed her

fortunes to California, New Mexico, Colorado, and Arizona. She was running a store, hotel, and restaurant in Tombstone when the Earps and Doc Holliday had their deadly date with the Clantons at the O.K. Corral. She left the American West for prospecting hot spots in Mexico and South Africa. When the call of the Klondike echoed around the world, her way of life was already established. Although regarded as a woman of advanced years — she was almost 50 — Nellie still had plenty of energy. She quickly organized an Alaska gold-mining company.

Once again, Nellie Cashman thought she had nothing to lose and everything to gain by heading off to the Yukon. There, in addition to being recognized as a successful prospector, she later earned a lasting reputation as an adventurous entrepreneur.

While Nellie Cashman was buying her train ticket to the West Coast, Marguerite Laimee was booking passage on a ship. She was leaving the gold camps of Australia on the first leg of her long journey to the Yukon. Having married at 14 and divorced at 16, Marguerite would never gain favour in polite society. Instead, she set off to follow the prospectors in far-flung locales, where her unorthodox behaviour was tolerated, if not encouraged.

Alone and anxious to make another new start, Marguerite arrived in Dawson City at the height of the rush in July 1898. She prospered in the bustling little riverside shanty town. However, Marguerite's greatest acquisition wasn't gold, real estate, or her profitable — but somewhat morally suspect — cigar-store business. It was her marriage to the man who was arguably the Klondike stampede's most important individual that brought Marguerite her greatest happiness.

Seeing the World

Kate Ryan's heart had been broken. Statuesque, buxom, and 22 years old, this six-foot farmer's daughter from Johnville, New Brunswick, had eyes only for Simon Gallagher. Alas, Simon was the son of a prosperous family. He had a very status-conscious mother. To head off what Mrs. Gallagher thought was a disastrous match, she convinced her good Catholic son to enter the seminary. She thought it better to be in the priesthood than to marry below your social position. Simon had the good grace to break the news to Kate himself. His studies meant he would soon be leaving the area, he told her.

"I'm leaving, too," Kate blurted. Now a rejected single woman of 22, Kate realized there was nothing left for her in the New Brunswick hamlet where she had been raised. Her mother agreed.

"Go, Kate," Anne Ryan urged as her daughter hesitated to board the train. "Here is your chance to see the world."

By September 1893, Kate was working in Seattle as a housekeeper and nanny for her mother's cousin. Two years later, she was training as a hospital worker. Back in Canada, and on her way to work at Vancouver's St. Paul's Hospital one sunny July day, Kate heard *Sun* newsboys shouting out the paper's stunning headline: "Gold in the Yukon!" Kate's imagination ignited. She was single and free of responsibility. She had saved a little money. Before the end of the year, Kate was inside the city's Hudson's Bay store, ordering supplies for her trip north. On February 28, 1898, Kate and her five grey huskies were standing on the deck of the steamer, *Tees*, watching the city slip away as they headed out of Seymour Narrows. It was the beginning of a year-long journey to the Klondike, and a life she had known only in her dreams.

Playing the Odds

Faith Fenton, the esteemed editor of *Canadian Home Journal*, had just been fired. When the publishers showed Faith the door, it wasn't because of lack of ability. It was politics, pure and simple. Despite a growing chorus of objections, Faith continued to support the new governor general's wife, Lady Eshbel Aberdeen, who insisted on advancing women's rights. It was the wrong thing to do in conservative Toronto.

The dismissal was a bitter professional blow to Canada's first female magazine editor and former Toronto reporter and columnist, whose name had become both familiar and trusted to tens of thousands of Canadian and U.S. magazine and newspaper readers.

Eleven years earlier in Ontario, known as schoolteacher Alice Freeman, Faith had convinced Barrie's *Northern Advance* to publish her slice-of-life series on lighthouse keepers and their families. Alice then succeeded in signing on at the *Toronto Globe* under the byline, "Faith Fenton." All the while, she continued her "real job" as a schoolteacher.

Old-age homes, women's prisons, orphanages, and hospitals were Fenton's beat as she researched her popular social-issue stories. She paid the price for her passion and confessed her doubt in a column: "A woman's bitterest moment, I think — especially if she be a woman unloved and therefore lonely — is when she turns from the mirror realizing for the first time that the fair flush of youth has vanished."

Now she had lost her job. The firing was a personal blow, as well as a professional setback. Three years earlier, Faith had finally given up her teaching job and taken the plunge as a full-time reporter. Now Faith was 40 and living on skimpy free-lance fees. She had nothing to lose by heading north. Happily, the *Globe* thought so, too, and made her their gold rush correspondent. Things were looking better already.

Chapter 3
Seekers and Runaways

I t wasn't always the lure of gold or the chance to earn a bigger income that goaded the women northward through the Alaskan mountain passes to the long, winding Yukon River. Some sought something else — aid for loved ones, a husband, an opportunity to grow and learn, or simply an adventure.

The Seekers

In certain cases, the special something Klondike adventurers sought was, in fact, a special someone.

Just before she was fired from her job as magazine editor, Faith Fenton had the good fortune to interview Canada's minister of the interior, William Ogilvie. Ten years earlier, while working as a surveyor, Ogilvie had spent time in the

Klondike, plotting the boundary between the Yukon and Alaska. Ogilvie privately assured Faith that marriage prospects were excellent in the Yukon. That was an understatement. In the Klondike, in 1898, men outnumbered women by at least 13 to 1.

Seven months after she stepped off the boat at Wrangell, Alaska, Faith succeeded in ending the "unloved and therefore lonely" existence she had once confessed to her readers. Ogilvie had become Yukon Commissioner, and as his private secretary, Faith had an inside track on Dawson's upper crust. She met John Nesbitt Elliott Brown, the territory's medical health officer and a member of the Yukon Council. The Fenton-Brown marriage on January 1, 1900, proved a fitting start to the new year's social swirl. The couple lived in Dawson until 1905, when Brown accepted a position at Toronto General Hospital. Very soon, Dr. John Brown's byline would be published far more often than Faith Fenton-Brown's.

* * *

Faith was just one of dozens of marriage-minded women who packed up for the Yukon. On the scent of a story, a *San Francisco Examiner* reporter faked a classified ad, claiming to be an anonymous prospector headed for the Yukon. The man invited a matrimonially inclined young lady or widow to accompany him. The enterprising journalist received more than 30 responses.

"I could be a helpmate to you," replied an 18-year-old husband-seeker whose family had all deceased, "and the union would be an advantage to me, for I find it a hard struggle in this world, without relatives."

"I don't look for perfection in any man; we all have our faults," one 28-year-old widow added solicitously. "I am willing to chance it — you, marriage, Alaska and all."

* * *

Five years before gold fever infected the world, veteran Alaska trader John Healy and his wife stepped off the train in Chicago. The couple had travelled thousands of kilometres from the far-off Yukon River gold hamlet of Forty Mile. Healy wasn't there for a holiday (besides, it would be months yet before the Chicago fair had its grand opening). Healy had come for one reason only: to raise money. Inside an office building he met an old Montana fur-trading associate, Portus B. Weare. Healy laid out his ideas for a Yukon River transportation company. There was much more gold to be found, he told his friend. Healy was sure that men all over the United States would be desperate for ways to get their hands on the gold. Weare invited the Healys to his fashionable home for dinner.

Bridget Mannion worked as a cook for Portus Weare and his family. She was in the kitchen when Healy regaled the Weares with exciting and colourful stories of his adventures at his isolated trading post at Dyea, located just a few

kilometres north of what was later to become the gold rush
town of Skagway. The family listened in fascination to Healy's
plans for transportation and the building of a new trading
post situated where the Yukon River met the Fortymile River.
Bridget was behind the kitchen door when she first heard the
words "Alaska" and "Yukon." The words — and the stories
around them — fired her imagination. Before long, the cook
approached the master of the house and told him bluntly
that she was off to Forty Mile.

"But you can't mine," sneered the incredulous Weare.

"That's true," Bridget admitted, "but there's them that
can …"

Weare's cook had no intention of mining. She had
arranged for Belle and John Healy to hire her as a domestic.
Bridget was after a husband, some lucky prospector who
would simply dig nuggets out of the ground for her.

More than a year later, a fashionable young woman
strode into Portus Weare's office. When he looked up, Weare's
jaw dropped. Then he took the elegantly gloved hand extend-
ed by his former cook. The name wasn't Mannion anymore,
Bridget informed him. At Forty Mile's first wedding ceremony,
Bridget had become Mrs. Frank Aylward. The wealthy couple
was off to Ireland to visit her family, and she had just stopped
by to say hello.

"Before I got 50 miles [81 km] up the Yukon, I had
received 125 proposals of marriage," she informed the astonished and delighted Weare. She held off, though, she said,

until she met "an engaging compatriot with a Kerry brogue and [a] mine that panned at the rate of $50,000 a month."

* * *

For Frances Dorley, a 26-year-old Seattle milliner and dressmaker who lived with her parents, life had become dull and uninteresting. With the arrival of the *Portland*, the city's residents had gone crazy. It must have seemed to Frances's worried parents that she had gone crazy, too. Frances might not have used the word "adventure," but that was clearly what the sheltered woman was seeking when she told her mother and father she was leaving the predictable life behind and travelling north.

Mr. and Mrs. Dorley opposed her rash plan. The fact that Frances was not travelling alone did not lessen their concern. Instead, when they realized that their daughter's travelling companions were three men, and that Frances had agreed to cook for them, their fears likely increased exponentially. Eventually they reached a compromise. Her folks finally agreed to give their blessing, but only on the condition that Frances return to her Seattle home (and therefore, her senses) in three weeks time. Frances quickly agreed.

Frances kept her part of the deal, but it was a fool's bargain. When she got a taste of the madness in Skagway, Alaska, the port-of-call for thousands of eager prospectors who were about to hike their way to the Klondike, she was a goner. Once home, she had barely unpacked before she began pestering her parents about travelling to Dawson.

Frances later conceded that her parents' concerns were justified. Nevertheless, she wrote, "after three weeks of insistent pleading, I finally won my mother's tearful consent and my father's reluctant blessing."

Frances Dorley sailed again for Alaska the following April. She married a Klondike doctor and made the Yukon her home for the next 20 years.

* * *

Meanwhile, San Francisco mother Georgia Hacker White was raising her children alone at a time when being separated from one's husband carried a particularly painful social stigma. The unrelenting needs of three young children kept Georgia housebound and nearly destitute. The Klondike gold rush seemed a unique opportunity. Georgia reluctantly made arrangements for her children to stay with friends in Nevada and with the Ladies' Protective Relief Society in San Francisco. Then she boarded the *Australia*.

Georgia's guilt and despair plagued her continuously. On the first exhausting leg of her journey to Dawson City, she poured out her anguish in her diary.

"I think constantly of my little ones and God knows at times it seems more than I can bear but I must — Oh, deliver me from becoming insane up here."

Georgia somehow found the strength to continue on, albeit briefly. Two months later, she was back in San Francisco, no wealthier than when she had left. However, the experience seemed to stiffen her resolve. She reclaimed her children and divorced her husband.

Georgia never did find financial fortune, but during that first voyage north on the *Australia*, she found something far more valuable — the love of a fellow passenger named Frank Mills. Georgia and Frank were married in 1902.

* * *

Anna DeGraf was a seeker of a different sort.

An economic panic in the 1870s had left the DeGrafs penniless in New York. Anna stayed with their young son and daughter while her husband went prospecting in Washington State. When she eventually decided to join him, Anna discovered that her husband had been murdered. The widowed mother somehow managed to start a dressmaking business in Seattle. Unfortunately, she suffered the fate of many business people of the time; everything she owned was destroyed by fire. Then her son disappeared.

On his departure, young DeGraf had promised his mother to return from Alaska in two weeks. Almost a month later, a stranger reported that he had seen him in the company of other young men in Juneau. Anna later managed to confirm this rumour.

At the time of her son's disappearance, Anna was 53. Instead of resigning herself to fast-approaching old age, Anna sold her business, packed up her sewing machine, and headed north to look for her missing son. She lived in Juneau for two years, anxious for any hint of his whereabouts. Then Joe Ladue, a trader and future millionaire who would soon establish Dawson City, reported seeing Anna's son near his sawmill at Ogilvie, on the Yukon River. So, in 1894, three years before the rush, Anna made her way to the Klondike. Her four-year search for her son proved fruitless.

Anna had returned to San Francisco and was living near her daughter when gold rush excitement reached its zenith. Once again, Anna — now 59 — made the arduous trek north. She was hoping against hope that gold fever had infected her long-lost son and that she would find him in Dawson City. Decades passed and Anna DeGraf never did find her missing son. What she found instead was the captivating lure of the North. The lure was so strong that it pulled her back again and again.

* * *

Many who ventured north simply sought to help others. Among them was a group of four women representing a brand-new medical aid organization, the Victorian Order of Nurses (VON). The brainchild of controversial Canadian social activist Lady Eshbel Aberdeen, the VON was initiated in honour of Queen Victoria's Diamond Jubilee. Concerned as much for their own reputations as they were for the welfare of their patients, doctors raised predictable howls of protest at Lady Aberdeen's unseemly concept. Nevertheless, the organization accepted its first recruits in the fall of 1897, just a few months before the gold rush presented the VON's Klondike contingent with a supreme test of fortitude.

Offering to send four nurses to the Klondike was a shrewd decision on Lady Aberdeen's part. Who could protest women who were willing to make incredible sacrifices to care for fathers, sons, and brothers in the northern wilderness? No pompous, pontificating doctor could compete with that kind of public relations. The nurses' departure, celebrated with a glittering farewell dinner at Aberdeen's governor general's residence, proved a wonderful opportunity to further the VON's cause.

As the train rolled out of Ottawa on its way to Vancouver, the four nurses had the pleasure of sharing their private car with none other than *Globe* correspondent Faith Fenton, who would help ensure that the VON continued to enjoy good press. The women had more company when they boarded the *Islander* in Vancouver: they were joined by the newly assembled Yukon Field Force, a military unit sent to bolster the overwhelmed North-West Mounted Police contingent.

Although it might have been a happy coincidence that the Field Force was on the trail at the very same time as the nurses, Eshbel Aberdeen recognized this stroke of luck and was quick to strike a bargain: military protection for her angels of mercy, in exchange for medical assistance for the 100 officers and men of the unit. While two nurses remained at the unit's Fort Selkirk headquarters, two others continued on to Dawson's Good Samaritan Presbyterian Hospital, which had opened in August.

The VON's work began on the trail as the nurses administered to military men and civilians they met along the way. It was a mild prelude to the horrors that lay ahead. With no sanitary system to serve its 18,000 residents, and little fresh food to feed them, Dawson was one of the unhealthiest centres in North America. The city's two hospitals were quickly filled to capacity. People suffered from scurvy, typhoid, venereal disease — the list went on and on.

"I thought I had seen something of typhoid fever, but nothing like this," one nurse wrote to Aberdeen. "Of severe haemorrhage cases, we had six at one time. Typhoid with pneumonia, with malaria, congestion of the liver, rheumatism, neuralgia, sore throat, discharge from the ears and sore eyes. Such sick men! Nor was the sickness all, but the filth and the vermin … Often a patient lay for days with only a blanket between him and the boards, thankful if we could give him a sack of shavings."

Accommodations for the two nurses in Dawson City were worse than those in the hospital. The women endured freezing temperatures while living in a small tent not far from the hospital. Before long one of the nurses took ill, and she was forced to undergo surgery in the log hospital's primitive operating theatre.

It is a credit to the unstinting efforts of these women that suffering was eased, men recovered, and, as one nurse told Aberdeen proudly, "not one of these patients had a bed sore or even a chafe, so closely were they watched and attended."

In another instance of self-sacrifice, an American woman named Lillian Oliver was intrigued by her friend's plan to venture to the Yukon. Lillian's husband was a sick man. She was desperate to make enough money to allow him to quit working. If her friend could chance a trip to the Yukon, perhaps she could, too.

"I saw in my mind's eye the vision of a proud wife bearing home to a long-suffering man the wherewithal to take him away from dreary toil and give his tired brain a rest," she imagined. "I was watching for the colour to come back to cheeks that had long been a stranger to it; I saw fire come to the eye grown dim; elasticity to steps grown weak; and happiness to both of us."

The Oliver couple's parting was heart-wrenching. The ailing husband asked God to keep his wife safe. He made Lillian promise that regardless of her success, she would return after no more than two years.

In Chicago, now a young socialite wife, Martha Black was intrigued. The ruby eyes of an ornate golden serpent seemed to move across her palm. Peering closely at her right hand, the great clairvoyant and palmist, Cheiro, intoned somewhat ominously, "You are leaving the country within the year. You will travel far. You will face danger, privation and sorrow." Martha smiled and stifled a mocking laugh. The young, happily married woman had every reason to think the palmist's predictions were altogether too outrageous.

Despite railroad strikes that exasperated and worried her father, Martha's economic future was secure. She had married handsome Will Purdy, son of the president of the Rock Island Railway. The vast fortunes of both families were large and would insulate the young couple from any personal suffering.

Even after the birth of her two sons, Martha's affluent, leisurely lifestyle continued much as before. She attended an endless round of concerts and plays, volunteered at the children's kindergarten, participated in outings with the cycling club (the bicycle-built-for-two was all the rage), and played euchre with the ladies after enjoying afternoon tea prepared by the Purdy family's servant girl.

The wealthy families' support of the Chicago World's Fair brought Martha into contact with the international who's who. Martha was chosen to be an attendant of Lady Aberdeen, who had been the unwitting cause of Faith Fenton's misfortune. The governor general's wife had raised funds for the Irish Building, and had travelled from Canada for its opening. There, Martha also met one of Lady Aberdeen's companions, none other than quick-witted and inquisitive reporter, Faith Fenton. Perhaps it was after meeting these dynamic women that Martha came to a realization: although she had every reason to be happy, something was missing from her life. Simply put, Martha Purdy was bored.

One day, Will Purdy came home full of plans to join the gold rush with a friend, Eli Gage. Martha's pulse quickened as she listened to Will's ideas. Eli, a banker's son who had just returned from Alaska, was married to a woman who had gold rush connections. One of the two stern-wheelers that had taken the newly rich prospectors to "the outside" just a few months earlier was named for Eli's brother-in-law, Chicago businessman and investor, Portus B. Weare.

Will and Eli planned to profit from their gold rush venture before they even left the windy city. They quickly purchased two ocean-going tugs, a steamer, and two sailing ships desperately needed to take gold-crazed hopefuls around Cape Horn to the Pacific coast. Martha and Eli's wife started packing.

Once they reached the Yukon, Martha would be no mere idle spectator. Her mission was to locate the claim of a long-lost uncle of a Rock Island employee. The old prospector had evidently willed his family the million-dollar proceeds from his Klondike claim. The employee entrusted the will itself to Martha, with the promise to pay her 50 percent of the proceeds once she had discovered the location of the golden legacy.

As soon as Martha climbed into the Pullman car for the train trip west, the palmist's prediction about her travels became reality. Martha might have paused to wonder about other things Cheiro had mentioned: "danger, privation, sorrow." Perhaps she pondered his final prediction: "You will have another child."

In Seattle, as the group prepared to board their steamer to Alaska, Will suddenly informed Martha that he had changed his plans: he was off to the Sandwich Islands (modern-day Hawaii). Martha was stunned. Will calmly waited for her to nod in agreement. Instead, it was his turn to be shocked. Incensed at his callous attitude, Martha told her husband he could go where he wanted, but she was off to the Klondike. Martha never saw Will Purdy again.

Running Away

The Klondike was the perfect destination for runaways who wanted anonymity. Virtually everyone was a stranger, mail delivery was sporadic, and telegraph wires had yet to be strung. Runaways could leave behind their previous names and the problems, fears, or concerns associated with their former identities. In the Klondike, the embarrassments, threats, and dangers of a previous life remained a secret.

On board the *City Of Columbia*, along with hundreds of matrimonial hopefuls who had booked passage from New York, was a woman who had absolutely no interest at all in finding a male companion. In fact, the woman who called herself Nettie Hoven had booked passage simply to escape an old love. Her live-in New York lover, John Mellen, was a dangerous man. He had threatened to kill Nettie. So she simply made up her mind to disappear, but it wasn't an easy task.

Nettie (most likely a false identity) was not a paying passenger. She worked as a ship's stewardess in exchange for passage around Cape Horn to Seattle. In the Straits of Magellan, the ship went aground.

"For three days and three nights we remained upon a rocky island in the vicinity of a cannibal village," the ship-wreck victim told an awestruck *Klondike Nugget* reporter once she finally reached Dawson City. "The natives were nearly seven feet high and very savage and we were constant-ly in fear of an attack." Fortunately, crew members patched the vessel, and the ship was able to round Cape Horn. They stopped again at Valparaiso for more extensive repairs, which were made at the expense of the near-destitute passengers. When the ship finally limped into Seattle, most had to end their trip. They had no more money. That didn't stop Nettie. She was determined to leave her old life behind.

Strolling the Seattle waterfront, Nettie saw a ship ready-ing itself for a trip to St. Michael, Alaska. She walked up the gangway, bag in hand, and boarded the ship. Nobody noticed Nettie on board the ship until they had started the trek, so she was forced to join the crew. By the time the ship reached Dawson City, Nettie had been travelling for seven months.

"I left New York without a cent," she told the *Nugget* reporter happily, "and reached Dawson with money in my pocket, so I think I aught [*sic*] to be satisfied." Nettie was satisfied, but she was not safe. Her vengeful lover was still on her trail. Once he arrived on the Yukon River, only the threat of action by the North-West Mounted Police and formal court documents could put the obsessed man in his place (which was anywhere but the Yukon), and bring Nettie peace of mind.

Whether they were motivated by the boredom of affluence, the agony of abject poverty, a shady past, the quest for adventure, or the desire to find gold (or a man who dug it up), in a sense, all of the hundreds of women who journeyed to the Yukon River were runaways. When the most exciting story of the decade hit the headlines, each seized the once-in-a-lifetime opportunity of the Klondike gold rush. Few had any idea just how far they would have to run to reach their destination, and most could not have imagined the horrors they would face on their journey.

Chapter 4
Routes to Riches

I t is likely that many women who began their journey to the Yukon had only the vaguest idea how they would reach their Klondike destination. Often it was just a day or two before they had planned to board a train or ship that travellers learned there were several routes to the riches. They might have wondered which route was best, but the more important question, if only they had known to ask it, would have been, "Which route is less horrific than the others?"

The All-American Routes
Those who chose to travel via American routes to the Klondike attempted to reach the interior gold fields from the head of Cook Inlet, where Anchorage, Alaska, is located

today. They would journey just below the inlet, through Prince William Sound at Valdez, or farther south over the coastal Malaspina Glacier. Americans chose these routes to avoid paying duties to Canadian customs. Few realized that by choosing these routes, they stood an excellent chance of losing their health, sanity, and even their lives.

Few of the 3,500 men and women who attempted to reach Dawson from the southern Alaskan port of Valdez succeeded. In February 1898, the weather along this all-American route was so terrible that frightened, sickened animals, including horses and dogs, had to be shot. Hundreds of stampeders were forced to become their own beasts of burden, pulling heavy sleds as they trudged through snow, sleet, and rain, and slid over treacherous ice. After nine exhausting kilometres, they had only just reached the edge of the towering Valdez Glacier that stood between Valdez and the Yukon. By August, when the ice and snow melted, the glacier was impassable. Travellers became snow-blind, they collapsed from scurvy, and went quietly — or not so quietly — mad.

The Rich Man's Route

Many women chose to travel the Bering Sea route. After leaving Canadian and U.S. ports, steamships ploughed north along the coast and turned east to St. Michael, Alaska. From there, travellers transferred to stern-wheelers for the long trip south along the Yukon River.

While offering the least strenuous way to reach the Klondike, the water route was also the most expensive. Stampeders who disembarked at Wrangell, Juneau, or Skagway, Alaska, could only watch with envy as other, more affluent hopefuls simply waved them goodbye and sailed on up the coast. Nettie Hoven, the young New Yorker on the run from her lover, was a fortunate exception. As the audacious woman worked for her passage around Cape Horn, Nettie enjoyed many of the benefits of the leisure class.

The sea voyage to St. Michael was a leisurely but tedious threeweek affair. However, when the two gold ships that sparked the rush arrived in San Francisco and Seattle in mid-July, even those who set out immediately scarcely had time to reach their destination before freeze-up. Once winter held the Yukon River highway in its grip, almost all travel ceased, as stern-wheelers became frozen in the ice. Passengers aboard such ships would either be forced to "winter over" for months in Circle City and other hamlets, or they could walk the rest of the way over the frozen river, against wind and snow, in temperatures as low as — 70 degrees Celsius. In the fall of 1897, just such an event occurred, and 1,800 early stampeders on board various stern-wheelers awoke to find that their vessels would not move again until spring break-up.

The Ashcroft and Stikine Trails
Many Canadian stampeders wanted to avoid customs duties applied when entering U.S. ports on the coast of Alaska.

Some chose the Ashcroft Trail, which ran more than 625 kilometres north through British Columbia, from Vancouver through the Cariboo and into the Yukon.

Only a handful of the 1,500 people who set out along the Ashcroft Trail reached their destination. Even fewer of the 3,000 starving horses, tormented by flies and mosquitoes, survived the trip. After months of exhausting travel, one hopeful finally reached the Stikine River, only to be told by the Native peoples that he would have to travel another 600 kilometres before reaching the gold creeks. The weary traveller reached for his gun and blew out his brains.

Of the thousands who first stepped onto the old wharf in Wrangell, Alaska, only a few hundred managed to set their packs down in Dawson City. In that small number were Kate Ryan, Faith Fenton, and the VON nurses. For these women, and thousands of men, the initial destination was the Stikine Trail.

To reach the Stikine, travellers disembarked at Wrangell, Alaska, and headed overland northeast to the tiny tent town of Glenora. Here, the Stikine and Ashcroft trails met. The word "trail" hardly described the slushy, mushy mess that men, women, and beasts slipped and slithered over as they journeyed north beyond the Stikine River, through Glenora and Telegraph Creek to Teslin Lake and their ultimate destination, the Yukon.

Four days after leaving Vancouver, former St. Paul's Hospital nurse Kate Ryan disembarked from a coastal steamer at the island port of Wrangell, Alaska. The intrepid young woman was bound for the Stikine Trail, where she would operate a series of canvas-roofed restaurants.

The first leg of her journey took her up the Stikine River in the desolate northwest corner of British Columbia. When Kate and thousands of others made the winter trip, river travel was treacherous. Deceptive ice on the frozen waterway led many to a watery grave. By the time Kate reached the small tent city of Whitehorse, the stout-hearted woman had been on the trail for more than a year.

A few months after Kate began her travels, the dauntless VON nurses, newspaper reporter Faith Fenton, and thousands of other gold-hungry travellers disembarked and began hiking along the treacherous trail. In the spring of 1898, Fenton, the VON contingent and the Yukon Field Force easily accomplished this leg of the trip. Travellers simply stepped aboard one of 17 paddlewheelers that plied the waters of the Stikine. When they stepped off at the trail head, the journey became more arduous. Faith and the nurses arose at 2 a.m. each day, and, as one nurse wrote, "went tramping, leaping, springing and climbing, a strain only the strongest and most sinewy women could bear."

Thousands had hit the trail, excited (and relieved) by news that Minister of the Interior Clifford Sifton had signed a tentative contract with builders to construct a 95-kilometre railroad from the head of the Stikine River to Teslin Lake. They would also employ a fleet of steamboats to sail placidly into the Yukon. The Senate balked at the cost. In the summer of 1898, work on the proposed railway was suddenly abandoned. Confronted with the muddy, narrow track that wound its way into the wilderness, bitter gold-seeking hopefuls scornfully labelled the proposed easy travelling route the "Stikine–Teslin Joke."

The Trails from Edmonton

Businessmen all over North America were eager to hitch their fortunes to the frantic quest for yellow ore. The good merchants of Jasper Avenue in the northern Canadian town of Edmonton were no exception. They eagerly promoted Edmonton as the "back door" to the Yukon. A Canadian guidebook told of a road that led from Edmonton to far-off Fort Selkirk on the Yukon River. The road was fictional.

"You don't need a couple of thousand dollars to start for the Klondike by the Edmonton route," calculated Joe Ladue, one-time Yukon trader and founder of Dawson City. A tireless Klondike booster, Joe had no hesitation in telling readers of his *Klondyke Facts*. "All you need is a good constitution, some experience in boating and camping and about $150."

About 1,500 stampeders left Edmonton for the Klondike. More than 70 died either on the trail or soon after their arrival in Dawson City. Some committed suicide. Others drowned or were injured; but most suffered the painful, lingering effects of scurvy. Only half who started out finally finished the trip, travelling more than 1,000 rugged kilometres before setting foot on Dawson City's Front Street. Among them was a gold-fevered Chicago couple, Emily Craig and her husband. It had taken them two years to reach their destination.

Like many American travellers, when the Craigs got off the train in Edmonton, they discovered there were many routes to the Yukon. A few days from town, most stampeders discovered the route they had chosen before leaving home had no discernable trail. "Hell can't be worse than this trail. I'll chance it," one suicidal traveller explained on a sign he tacked to a tree. His dead body was found beneath the message.

On the advice of their expedition manager, who purported to be experienced but had never actually travelled past the Chicago city limits, the Craigs chose the McKenzie Trail. One of the longest routes, it meandered across lakes and huge expanses of territory north of the Arctic Circle before running 1,500 kilometres south toward Dawson City.

As the only female of their group, the chore of cooking fell to Emily. After a day of backbreaking travel, the men's work ended, whereas Emily continued to toil over the campfire every night, feeding a less-than-appreciative gang of 13 men. Two months after they set out, the quarrelling group split up. Their manager abandoned the group and took their money.

The Craigs valiantly pressed on. By the time their ordeal was over, the couple had survived near-starvation, muskeg, and whitewater rapids. They had endured arduous portages that involved pulling heavy boats along on log rollers while sledding across the dangerous ice of Great Slave Lake. They spent two long winters at isolated outposts, and battled a fire that destroyed their tent and nearly all of Emily's clothing. After two years of exhausting travel, the Craigs finally reached their destination.

The Twin Passes
The cheapest, most direct routes to the Klondike wound through a pair of Alaskan mountain passes: the Chilkoot Pass and the White Pass. At their trail heads, the passes were less than five kilometres apart. During the Klondike gold rush, towns were built at the waterfront starting-points for each pass. Dyea became the jumping-off point for those braving the Chilkoot. It grew to a town of 10,000. Skagway became the lawless port-of-call for steamers disgorging hopefuls who then slogged up the White Pass.

Although longer, the White Pass had a gentler ascent. Stampeders could pack supplies on the backs of animals, rather than men. However, the route was new, and as the rain fell, the trampling of thousands of hooves, boots, and shoes turned the soft forest floor into a mire of muck. Animals became trapped in mud up to their bellies.

"My heart ached for ... the poor patient horses, burros, oxen and dogs that were bruised and bleeding until the trail was simply a trail of blood," recalled a 40-year-old divorcee who travelled up the White Pass with three other women. "The strain and hardships told on the men and many of them were cruel beyond description."

Impatient, gold-hungry men abandoned hundreds of starving, bargain-rate animals that they had bought in Seattle and Victoria. Hundreds more, their bones snapped by rocks, died screaming and snorting in agony. Others slipped and fell, or, as onlookers contended, simply walked off the trail's edge to smash themselves in the rocky gullies of Dead Horse Gulch.

Martha Purdy, Belinda Mulrooney, Ethel Berry, and Ethel's teenage sister, Edna "Tot" Bush, conquered the Chilkoot ordeal that proved impossible for so many others. These women and others battled against the odds to climb the pass and reach the Klondike: they simply persevered.

The Chilkoot offered a severe test of physical stamina that few stampeders — male or female — had ever endured, and no one who faced the Chilkoot would ever forget it.

"I was straining every nerve, every ounce of physical endurance in that ever upward climb," Martha Purdy remembered. "There were moments when, with sweating forehead, pounding heart and panting breath, I felt I could go no further."

"Stumbling ... staggering ... crawling ... God pity me!" she wrote many years later, reliving it all again. "Mush on ... mush on ... another breath! Another step ... God give me strength. How far away is the summit?"

Martha's brother, George, accompanied her on the trail. George attempted to comfort and encourage his sister. Finally his patience broke, and the exhausted man screamed,

Belinda Mulrooney and her group pause on the trail.

"For God's sake, Polly, buck up and be a man! Have some style and move on!"

Incensed, Martha "bucked up" and reached the summit.

Martha Purdy and other stampeders choosing the Chilkoot found what the former Chicago socialite called a "good wagon road" criss-crossing the milky-green Taiya River through the coastal rain forest. About 18 kilometres up the trail, conditions changed dramatically. From then on, Martha recalled, "we realized we were indeed on a trail of heartbreaks and dead hopes."

Belinda Mulrooney was among the first women to trek up Chilkoot Pass. The former steamship stewardess was operating the Juneau, Alaska, outlet for Seattle retailers McDougall and Southwick when she first heard about the gold strike in late 1896. Sensing the gold rush might make for a big business opportunity, the young entrepreneur quickly organized a group to head up the Chilkoot Pass. However, after reaching the trail, Belinda realized she had neither the men nor the resources needed for the trip. For a short time, she abandoned the project.

On April 1, 1897, four months before gold fever swept North America, Belinda returned to the pass, better equipped to meet the Chilkoot's main challenge — the formidable 45-degree climb from Sheep Camp to the mountain top. Just 2.5 kilometres from camp, the summit soared 1,100 metres into the sky, rising 300 metres in less than one kilometre.

Belinda discovered that it would be necessary to climb the so-called golden stairs many times. It was impossible to carry the necessary food and supplies in merely one trip. Stampeders had to climb the formidable slope over and over again, often making more than 30 trips and taking up to eight weeks of backbreaking effort to bring what was needed over the summit.

"Relaying was endless," Belinda recalled. "They'd make

one trip up to the top and knew they'd have to relay to get sufficient food for one year. Before they'd make the round trip they'd give up and say, 'impossible.'"

Always ready to seize an opportunity, Belinda took advantage of the daunting climb that defeated so many others.

"After our camp was placed, I got to buying supplies from the disheartened people who looked at the summit ... such a small percentage made the summit," she explained. "A great many returned, some snowblind, some ... sick or homesick." Belinda paid the desperate and dejected only a small sum for their supplies. Later, the opportunistic woman would charge much more in her Dawson City store for some of the same merchandise.

Georgia White, the California widow who had left her children behind, took comfort from a bottle as she climbed. By the time she and a friend reached the summit, the bottle was empty and they were light-headed, but they had conquered the pass. The last leg had taken them an exhausting 11 hours.

At Sheep Camp, Mae McKamish Meadows and her sharpshooter husband, Charley, pitched their tent and waited for their outfit to be packed over the summit. Within hours, mother nature turned nasty. At 6:30 a.m. one day, a landslide halfway up the summit let loose a torrent of mud and water on the unsuspecting camp below, carrying away tents, provisions, and supplies — including the Meadows' liquor and casino outfits — as well as the lives of three people.

"People saw the flood coming — could see a black dust and trees falling everywhere. No one thought it would be so bad," Mae confessed. "Charley went out, took a look … He came running in and said the flood was there and to run for my life."

Mae scrambled for her clothes and grabbed a small suitcase. The two narrowly escaped. "We were about 3 yards [2.7 m] away when the tent went down," she explained. "Well, I wanted to stop and see the water, and to try to button my clothes, but Charley kept saying to go on farther up, so I had to keep on running. If we had not got out at that moment we would have been drowned. It was terrible. Charley said if he had a Kodac [photograph] of me as I was running from Sheeps Camp flood, there would not be any use of going to the Klondike, as that would have been a gold mine in itself."

Not even Mae Meadows could make light of what happened near the same place the following spring.

In February and March 1898, storms dumped many feet of wet snow over the Chilkoot Pass. On April 2 and 3, many Chilkoot packers retreated to the lower reaches of the trail, below Sheep Camp. Soon afterward, less than two kilometres above the camp, hundreds of thousands of tons of snow broke loose and cascaded down the pass, obliterating the long lines of men and women struggling up the slope.

"Everybody rushed to the slide to help dig out those who were buried and were able to save some of them,"

Ethel Berry's sister, Tot, remembered. "A man and his wife were buried in the slide; she was taken out alive and directed them to where her husband was buried. They had just brought him to the surface when somebody yelled that another slide was coming and the workers all had to run for their lives. The rescued man was buried again and he wasn't found after the second slide."

Only a handful of victims were uncovered alive. Even while others attempted to rescue those who were trapped, the long line of stampeders had re-formed, and continued its painful shuffle up the slope.

In Sheep Camp, a long, white canvas tent was erected. A hastily scribbled sign near the front flap identified it as the morgue, which housed the frozen remains of dozens of victims. Estimates vary, but at least 70 people lost their lives in the Palm Sunday avalanche, enough to fill a new cemetery near Dyea. Many bodies were not revealed until weeks later, when spring temperatures rose and the snow receded.

Those who staggered to the top of either the Chilkoot Pass or the White Pass had little energy or inclination to reflect on their victory. Exhausted and aching, they might have felt beaten and defeated. Any celebration was tempered by the knowledge that they were still hundreds of kilometres from their Klondike objective.

Chapter 5
The Other Side of the Mountains

Weary trekkers trudged across the broad, treeless, rock-and-pond landscape of the summit. They were all numbed by the thought that, regardless of how exhausted they were, the journey had barely begun. Thousands of kilometres from their homes, every man and woman who had scaled the mountain faced a hard, bitter truth. Many days of travel — and who knew how many dangers — lay ahead before they would set foot in Dawson City.

The Way Down

"Then the descent! Down ever downward," Martha Purdy recalled. "Weight of body on shaky legs, weight growing heavier, and legs shakier. Sharp rocks to scratch our clutching hands. Snake-like roots to trip our stumbling feet!"

The vast land on the other side of the summit was dotted with a series of large bodies of water, beginning with Crater Lake at the very base of the mountain and Lake Lindeman a few kilometres north.

"The last two miles into Lindeman was the most excruciating struggle of the whole trip," Martha Purdy later wrote. "Rocks! Rocks! Rocks! Tearing boots to pieces. Hands bleeding from scratches. I can bear it no longer. In my agony I beg the men to leave me." Martha's brother, George, carried her in his arms for the final leg of the journey.

Martha and George made their trek in the summer. Travelling down the mountain was considerably faster — and certainly more exhilarating — in winter. The earliest stampeders merely slid their horses down the eastern slope of the Chilkoot. Men and women also slid down the slope, while those with heavily packed sleds exerted all their energy to keep their loads from running loose down the mountain. Tot Bush tobogganed down on a board, laughing with delight. Such momentary frivolity was merely a brief respite in an otherwise daunting journey.

The Tent Town of Lake Bennett

Crater Lake was small; Martha Purdy and many Chilkoot stampeders walked around it on their way to the Klondike. However, boating was another option. Boat building began in earnest on the shores of the first navigable lake in the

Yukon, the scenic 16-kilometre-long Lake Bennett. The voyage down the King River from Lake Lindeman into Lake Bennett was short, but furious nonetheless, as the white water of One-Mile Rapids churned along the river's twisting course.

Those who arrived at Lake Lindeman in the autumn of 1897 and 1898 had no time to enjoy the scenery. They were obsessed with the need to build a boat or flat-bottom scow quickly. It was a race against the calendar. Stampeders who knew nothing of carpentry or construction built flimsy crafts. Soon the river was littered with the remains of rafts, boats, and precious, water-logged possessions.

"There is not much time to rest or anything," Wild West performer Mae McKamish Meadows related to her sister in far-off Santa Cruz, California. "Do not know how long it will take to build two boats. May get a chance to write again … It is getting pretty late and it will take a lot of hurrying to get over the lake before it freezes."

In closing, Mae added, "Well, I must get out and see the town. I can hear hammers everywhere, it is the busiest little town I ever saw. People are hurrying off [to the Klondike] every day."

The "town" of Mae's letter was nothing more than a huge semicircle of white tents, stretching along the curving shorelines and dotting the lower reaches of the slopes. Soon tents covered both banks of the little river between Lindeman and Bennett. By May, the tent city of 5,000 boasted at least one legitimate street lined with canvas hotels, saloons, and doctors' and lawyers' offices.

Those who arrived later, walking through the small spruce grove high above the river, could hear the town before they saw it, the ringing of hammers and the rasp of saws greeting them up the slopes. As newcomers approached the crest of the hill near a half-completed church, trees were being felled all around them. Quite soon the lake-side banks were completely denuded. Sweating men carried or rolled freshly cut logs to curious-looking rough frameworks called Arm-strong sawmills.

One man stood perched on elevated scaffolding, holding the upper end of a long whipsaw, while his partner on the ground below gripped the other end. Up and down they heaved the saw, cutting through a newly chopped log only on the down stroke, the man above desperately trying to keep his balance while attempting to keep the saw blade along a straight line. The man below, standing in a blizzard of sawdust, tried to keep his temper in check. Dozens of partnerships ended acrimoniously on Bennett's Arm-strong sawmills.

Some parties paid other travellers to build their boats. Resourceful Belinda Mulrooney had come prepared, carrying the fibrous, oiled hemp used to make boats waterproof. "I had materials for boat building, and that stuff they pack boats with, oakum. All I had to do was to exchange that for labour. Pretty soon we had big boats all dolled up and named."

By 1898, commercial sawmills had been established. Martha Purdy and her party were customers.

"In three weeks our boat was finished," she wrote. "She was a fine unpainted craft shaped like a fisherman's dory and built of Alaska pine at King's Shipyard, Lake Bennett, at a cost of $275. She was 11-and-a-half metres across the bottom, and two-and-a-half metres at the top. In a short time our goods were loaded. When our several tons of luggage and our party of six got in, there was very little space above the waterline and very little room inside. However, we sailed away in drenching rain."

Down River to Dawson City

Staring out at the frozen surface of Lake Bennett in the early spring of 1897, Belinda Mulrooney felt she was racing against time. Once news of the strikes reached the outside, a tide of humanity was sure to wash up on Skagway and Dyea beaches. Belinda *had* to reach the Klondike quickly in order to be ready for business when the hordes arrived.

"We didn't wait for Bennett to be opened," Belinda explained years later. "We put the boats on the sleds and pushed on ... That lake stuff was easy going. There was quite a number of hours of sun and if the sleighs got stuck, we put a dog on to pull.

"When the wind filled the sails again the group simply unharnessed the dog, and threw him on the boat."

The following autumn, as Mae Meadows and her group

were building their boat at Bennett, summer sun showers turned to snow. Every passing day increased the risk that boaters would be trapped in a frozen river halfway to Dawson City. Men worked at a frenzied pace. Mae, Charley, and their companions finally pushed off the gravel beach on October 18, while others stood by and shook their heads in disbelief. It was a close call: the group got to within 50 kilometres of Dawson, but they awoke one morning to find the Yukon River frozen solid. Undaunted, they took the boats apart, built sleds, and pulled much of their gear down the frozen river and into the gold town.

Sledding down the ice should have been a fairly simple task, but the Yukon River surface was not the smooth skating rink most trekkers imagined it would be. Huge hummocks of ice formed as the surface thawed and refroze throughout the fall. Great ice pinnacles, often four metres high, dotted the eerie, white landscape.

Mae and Charley Meadows had skidded easily over the ice between Lake Marsh and Lake Laberge. By June, the ice had vanished, and the river seethed and foamed through two major white waters: Miles Canyon and White Horse Rapids.

In the spring of 1898, on their return trip to the Klondike, Tot Bush and Ethel and Clarence "C.J." Berry left a little too late to sled down the lakes. By the time the Berry party started out across Lake Laberge, the last link in the Yukon lake chain, the weather had warmed alarmingly. Less courageous souls would have put ashore, but the Berrys mushed on.

"We hugged the shore more closely each day," Tot wrote later. "As there was constant danger of the ice breaking, we carried long poles; in the case we should find thin ice the poles would prevent us from going through.

"When C.J. halted the sled to wait for us, he noticed that the runner was in water. Oh, boy! They used the whip on the dogs and worked like mad to keep the sleds moving. When Ethel felt the ice waving, she stopped, which was the worst thing she could do. Clarence looked back to see if we had noticed what was wrong with the sleds ... He couldn't leave the dogs and the sleds to come to her aid and so he yelled, 'For God's sake Ethel, *run!*'"

Tot grabbed her sister by the hand, and the two women dashed for shore. With each step, the heaving ice felt like "being on the ocean." Clarence had done the right thing in keeping the sleds moving. A dead weight would have gently opened the ice, swallowing everything, and possibly everyone. The next day, the group received a sober reminder of their narrow escape; a man and his dogs had gone through the ice not far away.

The ice began to move out of Lake Bennett on May 29, 1898. North-West Mounted Police Commander Sam Steele walked up the hill behind his office to see "the wonderful exodus of the boats." He counted more than 800 on the water that morning. Old-timers, who had made the trip through the lakes and down the Yukon River, doubted that many of the thousands of men who set off that morning and in the days that followed would make it to their destination. What chance did a woman have?

Not long after the break-up on Bennett, Commander Steele took a steamer trip through the lakes and down the Yukon River. At the little settlement of Canyon City, just a few minutes ride above the entrance to Miles Canyon, he learned from the local police detachment that more than 150 boats had been smashed in the river's rapids, and ten men had drowned. The police themselves had rescued a number of women and children, too.

Steele made a snap decision and decreed that no women or children would be allowed in boats on the canyon's three treacherous kilometres of rapids.

"If they are strong enough to come to the Klondike," he told an assembled crowd, "they can walk the five miles of grassy bank to the foot of the White Horse." For $25.05 per pound of cargo, a horse-drawn tram would portage a boat around the rapids.

Like all other stampeders, Martha Purdy and her group stopped at the North-West Mounted Police post on the short river between Lake Tagish and Lake Marsh. She was astonished to learn from a young policeman that during the past 12 months, 18,000 people had stopped for customs inspections. According to the police tally, Martha was the 631st woman to make her way to the Klondike.

Martha's group successfully navigated Miles Canyon before they were swept into the White Horse Rapids. For

Dwarfed by towering walls of basalt rock, travellers such as
Frances Dorley and Martha Purdy braved the churning water
of Miles Canyon, on the Yukon River.

some, the ride was exhilarating. One woman did it twice, just
for fun, saying afterwards, "I do not know when I ever enjoyed
anything so much in my life." For others, like Martha, it was
a heart-stopping experience.

"Half-way through, our steering oar broke with a crack
like that of a pistol shot, above the roaring waters. For a
tense moment, the boat whirled half her length about in the
current. Captain Spencer quickly seized another oar, calling
coolly, 'Never mind, boys! Let her go stern to.' A second's hesitation and our lives would have paid the penalty."

Frances Dorley, who had escaped her mundane Seattle

life and her cloying parents, had travelled nearly without incident, until she approached Lake Tagish. There she discovered that her "neat, expensive boat, made of soft cedar, was slowly coming apart at the seams." It was a common problem. Once ashore, the men she travelled with set to work reinforcing the boat, while plucky Frances "baked a batch of bread over a campfire and caught some fish." However, farther up the river, not far from the northern end of Lake Laberge, four rocky outcroppings rose high above the river's swiftly flowing waters. The resulting channels had been christened "Five Finger Rapids." Here Frances Dorley learned how little her prudent opinion mattered to her male companions. She had read a book in Skagway about the dangers of the river and how best to navigate through the Five Fingers. She suggested the group choose the channel farthest west.

"The little Scot, McChord, hooted at what he called my 'book-learned knowledge' and shouted that I, being a woman, could know nothing about navigation," Frances later wrote. "With true masculine loyalty, the other men sided with him."

As the boat tossed this way and that in the churning waters, discretion proved to be the better part of male valour, and two of the men quickly decided they had better row across to the safer channel.

"We all grabbed oars and began rowing frantically with all our strength," Frances reported. "We managed to force our way through the turbulent white foam until we were in midstream."

They were too late. Further exertion against the current was pointless. Mere seconds from the worst of the rapids, and with one huge island outcropping looming closer, another in the party suggested to the terrified group that they try to shoot through the centre channel.

"I closed my eyes, said a little prayer and tried to hold fast to my ebbing courage," Frances recalled. "Then we were shooting with brutal speed through the giant finger."

Miraculously, the flimsy boat and its passengers emerged from Five Fingers intact, and a few kilometres later, they easily manoeuvred through Rink Rapids. By this time, Frances and her companions had reached the halfway point in their Yukon River voyage. Once through the White Horse Rapids, the remaining river voyage to Dawson City would prove to be smooth sailing.

Despite the harsh conditions, horrific trails, and rushing rapids, many women made their way to the Yukon, and now they were ready to make a fortune.

Chapter 6
Leaving It All Behind

W hen women travelled to the Klondike, they often had little hint of the severe changes their lives were about to undergo. Quite apart from the brutal physical hardships of the trail, the women heading for the Yukon also endured unexpected psychological stress. Tolerance was stretched to the breaking point and dispositions soured. Behaviour became erratic as wilderness living conditions called into question almost everything the women had taken for granted during their former lives on the outside.

Klondike Fashions
One of the first visible signs of women's discomfiture was the sudden conflict over how they were expected — or how

they wanted — to dress once they disembarked from trains or steamships.

Decorous and voluminous, women's fashions were totally unfit for life on the trail. Vintage photos of Faith Fenton and the VON nurses show them sporting narrow-brimmed hats that were popular during the era. The women might have been in vogue on New York's Fifth Avenue, but in a place where practicality could mean the difference between life and death — or at least, between comfort and misery — these tiny hats were a symbol of the silliness of fashion.

Wide skirts that carefully hid everything but the soles of one's shoes were not designed for traversing deadfalls. Whalebone corsets that ensured a woman's "wasp waist," rendered their wearers breathless and faint after even the most modest exertion across streams and over boulders.

Ethel Berry and others made serious attempts to pack practical clothes. In her bride's trousseau, she packed articles made of "good, strong, warm, substantial material that could stand the wear and tear of a year, and maybe more, in that bitter cold country." Ethel's choices were undoubtedly influenced by her new husband, Clarence, who had lived in the Yukon for years. Few had the advantage of insight.

In Juneau, Belinda Mulrooney gained insight from conversations with men who knew the Klondike. As a result, she had some of her wardrobe and an eider-and-fox-fur sleeping bag custom-made in Seattle. Along with "short" calf-length skirts and men's-style shirts, Belinda also had the prescience to pack snow glasses to diminish the glare that left many stampeders blind.

"I ditched the corsets," she recalled, "which was a rash thing to do in those days. I suffered a lot from the whalebone stuff. I always had a grudge against it."

While still in Chicago preparing for her trek, Martha Purdy tried to make practical wardrobe choices, one of which was "a skirt of shockingly immodest length (it actually showed my ankles)."

Yet Purdy's own social status dictated that, as part of Chicago's upper class, she also include, as she put it, "a blouse with a high stiff collar almost to my ears, and a pair of voluminous brown silk bloomers, which came below the knee." In an age where the sight of an ankle was provocative, all prudent women wore bloomers, or knickers, under their skirts. The baggy pants guarded against the accidental exposure of shapely white flesh. Once on the trail, these women railed against social convention and the customary confining, concealing clothing.

Within a day or two of her arrival in the Yukon, Martha gave up many of her fashionable clothes. "I shed my sealskin jacket," Martha confessed. "I cursed my hot, high, buckram collar, my tight heavily boned corsets, my long corduroy skirt, my full bloomers which I had to hitch up with every step."

Gold rush veteran Nellie Cashman did the unheard-of: she wore pants. Nellie really didn't care what anybody else thought. She had been in more gold camps than most of the men who raised their eyebrows at her. She knew better than they what worked and what didn't.

By the time winter turned to summer on the Teslin Trail, Kate Ryan had exchanged her dogs for horses. Kate created a tough, culottes-style riding skirt, so she could swing her leg over her mount and ride comfortably, like a man. She shortened her long mackinaw coat so that it, too, fit well while she rode on horseback. A practical, broad-brimmed straw hat which she called her "cow breaker" shaded her face from the summer sun as she led her string of pack horses up the trail.

Predictably, many men were less than enthusiastic about these deviations in dress. In Wrangell, *Globe* reporter Faith Fenton was scolded by a U.S. army officer who objected to the length of her practical, knee-length skirt. Properly chastened, Faith sought out a seamstress who lengthened the skirt to her ankles. Ironically, as black satinette was the only material available for the job, the result had a more risqué effect than the original skirt.

By 1899, weary Edmonton trail veterans Emily Craig and her husband had finally arrived on the Yukon River. They booked passage on a paddlewheeler bound for Dawson City, where civilization's trappings had arrived some time before.

After their disastrous tent fire, Emily's husband had purchased a beaded buckskin dress, fur cap, and moccasins from the Native peoples to replace Emily's worn clothing. Warm and wear-resistant, it was the perfect outfit for the rugged wilderness. As they waited for the steamer, Emily saw other women on their way to "the city."

"It was a sight to see the dresses and hats that the ladies, going through here, were wearing," Emily later remembered. "There was no white woman's clothing in these parts, and it seemed everyone was looking at me. I wanted to cry, but that would not make it any better … and I wanted some new dresses before I got to Dawson."

Less than a month earlier, the ceremonial last spike of the White Pass and Yukon Railway had been driven into the rail tie at Lake Bennett. Now women bound for the Klondike could simply lift their long, fashionable dresses and step daintily up the black, iron steps of a Skagway train coach. They would sit in comfort, looking down at the deserted pass that so many exhausted stampeders had tramped through just months before.

Rustic Hospitality

In the late summer of 1897, John Feero, who had decided to escape financially depressed Washington State, was finally reunited with his wife, Emma, and their five children in Skagway. John had decided to return to the transportation business. The market was strong; men were desperate for pack animals. John was thriving in the tent town's rough-and-ready atmosphere. When finally reunited, the family went to a big, barn-like two-storey building for a celebration dinner. The "hotel" featured a makeshift dining room with long tables and benches. The cloakroom was nothing more than a long bench with nails in the wall.

After dinner, Emma wondered where they were to sleep. John pointed to a ladder leading to the floor above. "Huh! I can't walk up that ladder!" Emma protested primly, but to no avail. It was either go up the ladder, or spend a sleepless night below. When she finished her climb, she found that nothing but canvas curtains divided the loft into rooms. Three mattresses were scattered on the rough floorboards. Surrounded by drunks on both sides of the canvas curtains, it was a sleepless night for Emma in her second-storey "bedroom."

Before breakfast, Emma looked down the ladder at the unshaven mob slurping and munching below, and she told John, "I can't go down there." She quickly discovered that she must join the mob or go hungry, so down she went.

Farther up the trails, hospitality was just as crude, and hotel accommodations were even more rustic than those in Skagway. During her group's descent from the summit, Martha Purdy took supper at a cabin. She had come a long way, indeed, from china-and-crystal dinners served by the hired girl in the comfortable Chicago home she had shared with her former husband, Will. Two dollars in the cabin bought bean soup, ham and eggs, prunes, bread and butter, and an apology from the proprietor.

"The middle of it ain't done," he admitted, gesturing to the bread, "but you don't have to eat it. I hurried too much."

Martha's brother, George, carried her into the Tacoma Hotel at Crater Lake, and she stumbled off to a "canvas stretched on four logs, with a straw shakedown." Yet Martha was so exhausted that she later confessed, "The downiest couch in the world or the softest bed in a king's palace could not have made a better resting place for me."

Others toiling up the "trail of blood" known as the White Pass would have been envious of Martha's modest comfort. After an arduous 14-kilometre hike, one woman asked a fellow stampeder how far she had to travel to reach the White Pass Hotel.

"Why, bless your blue eyes," the man laughed, "There it is, a hundred feet [31 m] ahead!"

"Oh, is that it?" asked the incredulous trekker. "I thought it was horse stable or pig sty!"

Once inside, the woman asked the manager to show her to her room, as she was very tired. Her request was greeted by guffaws from the men sitting around the tables.

"Well, Miss, I've only got these two rooms," the landlord explained patiently. "One is the kitchen, the other is a barroom, dining room and settin' room. You'll have to sleep here if you stay."

She and her companion were soon joined by three other exhausted women. The owner spread blankets on the rough plank floor, and they all slept side by side — "five women with our heads under the bar."

Had the White Pass Hotel's proprietor heard about this

exchange, he undoubtedly would have been amused. He was none other than John Feero, whose wife, Emma, had been so disgusted by her own hotel experience in Skagway just a few months earlier.

Hearth and Home

Most husbands and fathers missed their wives and families; however, many stampeders or frontier businessmen concluded that it was far better if "the missus" and little ones remained thousands of kilometres away from the crude northern existence. Though there are no records of his feelings, life was never the same for John Feero after Emma and the children arrived at Skagway. John led his family to the woods behind the beach-front area that would soon be divided into boardwalk-fronted streets. The "residential area" was a collection of canvas tents scattered haphazardly among the trees. John's tent was staked out just a few metres from the horses he packed.

Emma had managed to bring three mattresses and two box springs up the coast. Inside the large tent, two mattresses were placed on boxes, and the other went on posts hammered into the dirt floor. Now the family had an under-the-bed storage space. Emma had also brought a stove, which was placed in a corner of the tent. There was no table, so John dutifully bought lumber to make one. Even though the sawmill worked non-stop, there was not a board to be bought. Instead, John and others drove four posts into the floor, over which he nestled a rented wooden box. John went into the woods to saw the ends off some logs. Now the family had chairs. Before long the family's cabin had been hacked out of the trees, and they began to enjoy the rustic comforts of home.

The Classes Mix and Mingle

Gold fever knew no class distinction. The lust for gold and the opportunities it brought cut across every social class and ethnic background. People of high social and financial positions (including the Seattle mayor, who abandoned his office without notice) headed for the Klondike with the same zeal as retail clerks and near-penniless labourers. When they sailed away up the coast or tramped along overland trails, men and women abandoned the barriers that kept various social classes from interacting along anything but acceptable pathways. For decades before the rush, hardy fur traders and a small number of prospectors had formed friendships and alliances with the Native peoples they traded with. The quest for gold also brought together stampeders and Native peoples. Soon lonely, isolated men sought native women as personal partners. The fates of some of these women were inextricably bound to the gold rush.

While at Lake Laberge, Frances Dorley's party came upon a group of Native people selling trout to gold seekers. As members of the group clustered around to examine her, she immediately grew concerned.

"Finally," Frances reported, "the chief spokesman of the group stepped forward and addressed my companions: 'Nice squaw. We like her. Which one of you does she belong to? We give you many fish and even much money, if you will leave her here with us.'"

One of the men came to Frances's rescue.

"Stepping between the Indians and me he murmured nervously that I was his squaw and not for sale," Frances later recounted. "I, the 'fine squaw,' stood rooted to the spot, feeling more afraid than at any other time since leaving Seattle."

George Carmack, the man whose strike started the rush, married a Tagish woman who died soon after their traditional marriage ceremony. George's mother-in-law then arranged a marriage between George and his dead wife's younger sister, Shaaw Tlaa, whom he called Kate. For years, they were happy. Together they packed outfits from John Healy's trading post up the Chilkoot. Later, Kate managed the trading post George built near Five Fingers Rapids (at the site of present-day Carmacks).

When George became rich, Kate, as his partner and the mother of their daughter, Graphie, became rich, too. Kate's riches — and her happiness — ended in 1898, when she accompanied her cousin, Tagish Charlie; her brother, Skookum Jim; and George to the outside for the first time.

While in Seattle and San Francisco, George's native partners and wife became victims of culture shock — and the affects of liquor. All three were jailed on drunk-and-disorderly

Kate Carmack, in a California studio portrait, wears a heavy gold "nugget" necklace, a symbol of the Carmacks' new-found wealth.

charges. As a man attempting to establish himself in California business circles, George was disgusted. His reputation was at stake. Before long he had separated from Kate and had bought out Charlie and Jim. Kate attempted to sue for alimony, and later, child support. Still unsuccessful after years of legal wrangling, Kate moved back to what is now Carcross to live near friends and family. Making native handicrafts for visitors and living on the edge of poverty, Kate was the most visible victim of the clash of cultures brought about by the gold rush.

With the arrival of more "white women" to the Klondike,

attitudes changed quickly. Most of the women didn't want to associate with the Native peoples. Scores of early prospectors abandoned their native wives. It was simply too unseemly for a white man to be seen living with a native woman. In 1905, when the wife of the Anglican bishop gave a visiting Mayo woman a place of honour at a church tea, auxiliary members were scandalized.

Before John Feero began building his cabin, his wife, Emma, noticed that someone was building on the next lot. Emma was delighted to have neighbours nearby. The family would have company. The happy anticipation was short lived. The next morning, Emma was outraged to see a large saloon sign on the roof of the neighbours' cabin. Emma forced John to buy the building to avoid living next to a saloon and the class of men she thought it would likely attract.

Effrontery often began on overcrowded ships sailing up the coast. Martha Purdy had booked a stateroom with three berths. When she walked in, she saw others' bags on the floor. Obviously, some mistake had been made.

"I was soon told that I was to have company," Martha recounted. "The double lower had been allotted to a tinhorn gambler and his female companion, the middle to me and the upper to 'Birdie,' destined to be one of the most notorious characters of the Klondyke. My brother George and I protested to the captain and purser, but … In the language of today, 'we could take it or leave it.'"

Martha took it.

Less than two years after arriving in Dawson City, working first as a merchant, then as a restaurant operator, and later as the owner of two hotels, Belinda Mulrooney had become one of the best-known entrepreneurs in the North. She agreed to accept donations for the city's most prestigious fund-raising event, a benefit for St. Mary's Hospital. The town's dance-hall girls and prostitutes, who were as likely to be hospitalized as anyone, wanted to contribute. The money was collected, then given to Belinda's friend and Chilkoot trail-mate, Joe Barrette.

"Good God, Joe!" Belinda exclaimed when he told her who had contributed the donation. "What will I do with this? I can't account for this." She told Joe he had better give the donation back, explaining, "they'll think it's dirty money."

Joe took the comment literally, and he decided to "get all gold dust. That's clean enough."

Belinda shook her head. "It's not that. It's where it comes from. You take it back."

"No, I can't do that," Joe argued. "Fine women! Give to churches! Good as anyone! I know it! You know it. Make the rest know it."

Belinda accepted the donation, and she labelled it "a gift."

"That was all the information they could get out of Joe or me," Belinda added. The gift was worth $20,000.

In the Klondike, the mixing and mingling of the classes was short-lived. Within months of its founding, Dawson

City began to develop its own obvious class system. The re-establishment of a familiar social ladder — judges and civil servants on the top rung, prostitutes on the bottom rung — was comforting to most newcomers, who never really felt at ease in the company of any other than "their own kind." Still, after well-established social barriers were broken, many women were never the same again.

"Polly, what will people think of you if you talk like that when we get home?" whined Martha Purdy's brother, George, when he heard her rough, gold-creek language.

"Think of me?" Martha scoffed. "If I get my half-million I won't give a damn," she retorted, still hopeful that she would find the long-lost fortune she had come to the Klondike to locate. "And if I don't," she continued hotly, "then they won't give a damn for me!"

Chapter 7
A Wife's Duty

F ollowing news of big strikes in the Klondike, husbands and wives throughout North America argued about whether or not they should try their luck in the North. Thousands debated over the life-changing decision: should the husband go to the Klondike, or simply keep his job and carry on? If he went, should the wife go, too? In the face of this madness, they had to determine what a wife's real duty was: to stay at home with her children, or to support her husband on the trails.

Only three percent of the 28,000 stampeders who journeyed to the Yukon were women, which suggests that most wives agreed to stay thousands of kilometres behind and carry on alone. A few men managed to persuade their wives to accompany them on what many regarded as the grandest adventure of all. Some wives persuaded their husbands to let them tag along, saying the men would not, or could not, go alone. Ethel Berry told a reporter, "I went because my husband went and I wanted to be with him."

Till Death (and the Klondike) do Us Part
Wives and mothers who decided to "Ho, for the Klondike" also had to decide if their children should join the trek. For many, the answer to that question was an agonizing, "no."

"My sweet, darling Kidlets," one bereft mother wrote from Dawson to her children in far-off New York City. "Being apart from you ... is the greatest trial I have to endure, and I try very hard to keep from thinking of home and sometimes a few days pass away and I do not look at [the photo of] your sweet faces, because I know my courage and endurance give way ... I do not think I will write very much more." She closed the letter with, "as the tears blind me ..."

Few couples travelled with their young children, and some of those who did wished they hadn't. At least three children were buried on the Chilkoot Trail: one at Dyea and two at Lake Lindeman. Children were particularly susceptible to the hepatitis, meningitis, and typhoid that ravaged the trails and Klondike settlements during the gold rush.

Not long after she and her brother, George, had built a log-cabin home across the Klondike River from Dawson City, Martha Purdy made a shocking discovery. Her estranged husband, Will, had given her a going-away gift. She was pregnant.

Martha Purdy, her brother George, and the little "cheechako" (meaning "tenderfoot"), in the cabin above Lousetown.

"I could not believe it. I would not let my mind dwell upon it," she admitted later. "Terror-stricken, I faced this Gethsemane." In her condition, Martha knew she could not face the long trail to the coast again. She sought help. Father William Judge, the so-called Saint of Dawson and founder of St. Mary's Hospital, told the impoverished mother-to-be it would cost $1,000 to deliver her baby, a sum that was more than the average wage-earner's annual pay. Judge was an aggressive fund raiser, and perhaps he knew Martha came from a wealthy family. He even offered to wait until spring for payment. Instead, Martha decided to deliver the child on her own.

"And weren't the menfolk surprised when they returned from work at night, to find, wrapped in red flannel — a fine, healthy baby boy!" Martha remembered proudly. "They called him the little cheechako." Martha named the boy Lyman, after her grandfather. Soon Martha realized that even the men on the trail missed their children back home.

"What a welcome the camp gave my baby! The men in our party, and my neighbours, all men, took full charge. They kept the fires going. They brought in foodstuffs — fresh-baked bread, cakes, chocolates, ptarmigan, moose meat, every wild delicacy of the country. Miners, prospectors, strange uncouth men called to pay their respects."

During their first few weeks in the Klondike, newlyweds Ethel and Clarence Berry made their meagre home in Forty Mile, a few kilometres north of what was to be Dawson City. There was no gold to be found in the muddy tracks between the stores, warehouses, and saloons of the little village. So, not long after they had arrived, Clarence left again for the creeks. Ethel was alone in a dismal little log settlement full of rough-and-ready strangers. She had never been alone before.

"There was nothing, absolutely nothing to do," she discovered to her dismay. "Just imagine sitting for hours in one's home doing nothing, looking out a scrap of window and seeing nothing, searching for work and finding nothing." Ethel was reduced to walking to a nearby cemetery "for consolation."

Soon, however, Clarence was back in Forty Mile. He'd

found no gold, and he had eaten through his outfit. The couple was broke. Actually, their financial distress was a blessing in disguise, because it put cash-strapped Clarence behind the bar of Bill McPhee's saloon. He was on duty, pouring drinks and washing glasses, the fateful night that George Carmack strutted in with his incredible tale of a huge strike.

Others were skeptical, but within an hour, Clarence had arranged a grubstake with Bill McPhee and off he dashed to tell his wife the news. As soon as he was able, Clarence was rowing upriver, determined to be among the first to stake a claim along the creek. The next morning, Forty Mile was a veritable ghost town.

Ethel played a critical role in Clarence's plan. Clarence quickly returned to Forty Mile, having registered his claim at Fort Constantine, the nearby North-West Mounted Police post. He threw into his rowboat as many supplies as it would carry, telling Ethel to bring the rest — and herself — on the next available paddlewheeler. He dashed off again. When the little steamer, *Alice*, nudged against the bank a few days later, Ethel was informed she had 12 hours to get her supplies together for loading. How would she know how much food, clothing, and equipment to bring for the coming winter months? She put together about *five tons* of supplies before the appointed departure time.

Before the year was out, the Berrys would be millionaires. But their happily-ever-after story was the exception rather than the rule. The horrific conditions and unremitting exhaustion were enough to end hundreds of partnerships between men. Trying conditions proved destructive to marital partners, as well.

Not long after 1898's spring break-up, 1,000 vessels lay becalmed on Lake Laberge. Suddenly there was an unexpected gust of wind. Sails snapped and fluttered, and boats jerked this way and that. A woman standing in the stern of one particular scow lost her balance and tumbled into the chilly waters. One of the two men on board raced to the centre of the scow to lower the sail, expecting the other man — the woman's husband — to dive overboard and come to her aid. Instead, the husband panicked and began racing about frantically, screaming for help.

Two prospectors in a nearby boat witnessed the mishap. The steersman dropped his tiller and dived to the woman's rescue. He quickly assisted her to his boat and, with the help of his partner, brought her aboard. The scow, meanwhile, had drifted some distance away, so the rescuers rowed over, reuniting the woman with her husband. To their astonishment, the woman announced to her husband — and to everyone within earshot — that she had all of *him* she wanted. She turned and pointed a finger at her shivering rescuer.

"If this man will take me, he can have me," she shouted. The steersman knew a good thing when he saw it.

"Yes, I'll take you," he shouted back.

The steersman's companion wasn't so sure he liked the idea of an unexpected third partner, even one as comely as the woman in question. He made his feelings clear. The rescuer dove under the boat's canvas for his outfit, re-emerged with a six-gun, and levelled it at his wide-eyed partner. The woman was under his protection, he informed his partner. Then, without taking his eyes off his partner, he shouted to the woman's devastated husband to throw her belongings into their boat. The woman reportedly got a divorce from the panicky husband and married her rescuer, to the admiration of everyone who witnessed the incident.

Keeping the Fires at Home Burning
Conditions in the Klondike were different in almost every respect from those on the outside; however, somehow the traditional roles of men and women were maintained. Ironically, the brutally tough work that engaged the men on the creeks helped ensure that their wives remained back at the cabin, attending to domestic duties. Men simply didn't have the time or the energy.

Most women were stunned by the paucity of food items available. After Martha Purdy finished making her rude, one-room log house a home, she set about keeping house for George and became hostess to many of his working companions.

"Much against the will of the party," she remembered, she had carried into the Yukon "two linen tablecloths, with two dozen napkins, silver knives, forks and spoons for company." She discovered that food shortages, coupled with outrageous prices, made for a meagre Klondike larder.

"For six months we were to be entirely without butter, sugar or milk," Martha recalled. "Our breakfast consisted of cornmeal mush with molasses and clear coffee. How I longed for a change of diet — some fruit and vegetables!"

There were hundreds of other shortages, as well. The midnight sun was a blessing in the summer, but the near endless dark of winter was a dreadful curse for hundreds of men who could not afford artificial light. Martha remembered, "After the supper dishes were done, if I sewed, as a special favour, I was allowed two candles."

In the spring of 1898, Tot Bush, Ethel Berry's sister, joined Ethel and others in the family on their return trip to Klondike. Tot's introduction to the domestic drudgery that she would experience in Eldorado Creek began on the Chilkoot Trail itself. There was scarcely any sign of the huge wealth the Berrys were bringing up from the dirty depths below.

"It was hard work cooking for so many with the same kind of food every day and so few utensils," Tot wrote later of her time in Sheep Camp. "Ethel and I did the cooking for our crowd. We had to set up everything twice for each meal, as we didn't have enough dishes." However, she added proudly, "the cooking smelt so good to strangers passing the tent that they would poke their heads in to ask if it was a boarding house."

A Wife's Duty

A year earlier, in the crazy summer of 1897, when Ethel and Clarence had returned to civilization from their multi-million-dollar claims on the Eldorado Creek, they had been besieged by the press. The Berrys fled Seattle and headed to San Francisco, where they were finally interviewed by reporters and authors. None of the wives on the creeks described their homemaking challenges better than Ethel.

"We could not get one drop of water without first melting the ice, which necessitated keeping a fire all day," Ethel told reporters. Keeping the fires at home burning was no mean feat, either.

"Keeping the fire is enough to occupy the whole of one person's time," she assured *San Francisco Examiner* readers. "The wood is full of pitch and blazes up and is out again almost before one can walk across the room and back." Provisions were often kept in caches, small elevated log enclosures located outside the cabin. This crude food preservation system presented another problem. "All our supplies which we kept in the cache had to go through the same process of thawing before being cooked."

Author A. C. Harris wanted to know what the ladies of the Klondike did for fun. He got an earful.

"We never felt like playing games or going in for any kind of amusements after the day's hard work was done," Ethel told Harris. "We did not think of anything but sleep and rest. That was the main reason we did not die of homesickness. We had no time to think!"

A reporter asked Ethel if she had advice to give women headed for the Klondike. Ethel replied without hesitation, "Oh, stay away, of course!" Many female newspaper readers undoubtedly heeded her words and abandoned any plans they may have had to go north. Many others who braved the trails and the trials of the Yukon fervently wished they had done the same.

Chapter 8
Making Their Way

After surviving the long and arduous journey to the land of the midnight sun, the real work began. Many had come to the Klondike in search of financial freedom and independence. For those who expected to dig up gold and go home rich, the first few days in Dawson City and on the creeks were a painful shock. Even for 1897's first arrivals, there were few claims left to stake.

For most, finding work (at least, legitimate work away from Paradise Alley) proved almost impossible. However, for those who could overcome the fear and fatigue, there were opportunities waiting.

Cashing in on the Masculine Market
Soon after tents were raised along Dawson City's river bank,

women found financial success, opening a host of businesses such as restaurants, laundries, and baths, where many men parted with their gold in return for goods.

Anna DeGraf hefted a sewing machine across the Chilkoot more than once. She never lacked work, sewing furs for the Alaska Commercial Company in Circle City, and then, during Dawson's heyday, sewing costumes for the dance-hall girls at the Orpheum Theatre. She also created cold-weather clothes for the North-West Mounted Police. At one time, Anna employed at least four other women in her workshop. The widow was far too busy to contemplate marriage, although she received at least two proposals. Anna was also successful at staking many claims. She received numerous tips about open claims, and she would stealthily wander up the creeks in the dead of night to hammer in her stakes before competitors arrived at dawn.

* * *

Having left Seattle, Frances Dorley was determined to stay in the North. After three months of searching, Frances found a cabin near the burgeoning town of Grand Forks, at the junction of the Bonanza and Eldorado creeks. She converted the building into a roadhouse for weary travellers.

"I baked tons of bread and pies and made millions of doughnuts," she recalled. Butter arrived in five-pound wooden buckets. Once she had emptied them of their original contents, Frances filled them with baked beans.

By spring, Frances was searching for a partner to share the workload. In Dawson she met Mrs. Moore, a middle-aged widow. Together the two women turned the Professional Men's Boarding House into a riproaring success.

As she had done in so many other gold camps, Nellie Cashman turned to food service for an income base, and she opened The Can-Can in the early summer of 1898. By the fall, she had opened the Cassiar Restaurant. However, her most memorable business venture was in the area of fund development. Nellie was legendary for her philanthropy, which she had begun in British Columbia years earlier. There she provided tender care to prospectors who gave her the nickname, "Angel of the Cassiar." A few weeks after arriving in the Klondike, Nellie was walking the creeks, asking prospectors to dig deep for an expansion to St. Mary's Hospital.

A tender-hearted woman, Nellie looked and sounded like a tough-talking gold-field veteran. Her relationship with prospectors was a unique one. "Men are a nuisance," she complained good-naturedly to an interviewer. "Men — why, child, they're just boys grown up. I've nursed them, embalmed them, fed and scolded them, acted as mother confessor and fought my own with them and you have to treat them just like boys."

Kate Ryan was, perhaps, the best-known restaurateur on the Stikine Trail. Initially, the former nurse fed members of the North-West Mounted Police, and later she opened a Glenora restaurant. After two years of travel, Kate finally arrived in

Canada's newest railway town, Whitehorse, where she quickly opened Kate's Café. Here Kate's life took a unique turn.

Soon after her arrival, the North-West Mounted Police called on Kate to take a job as prison matron. Gold smuggling had become a concern, and the Canadian government required a female gold inspector. Formidable-looking Kate was the only serious candidate for the position. She accepted a post as constable special, designed her own uniform, and began riding the trains and the steamers, asking passengers if they had any gold to declare.

On board a steamer docked at Whitehorse, Constable Ryan's question was greeted by indignant silence from one fashionable woman. Kate repeated the inquiry, but to no avail.

"I'm sorry madam, but if you do not answer the questions, you will have to be searched."

"Oh, scarcely," came the haughty reply. "Do you know to whom you are speaking? I am the wife of Major General Gerald Brompton of the United States Army."

"And I, madam, am myself an officer of the British Crown. Would you kindly step into the cabin?"

Moments later, the woman had literally let down her hair, reluctantly exposing a number of carefully concealed nuggets.

There were big profits to be made on Dawson City's seamy side. Within four months of her arrival from the Australian gold fields, unorthodox Marguerite Laimee opened the first of two Dawson cigar stores, which were merely fronts for bawdy houses. Traffic was so good that she poured $30 in gold into her pokes each morning from floor sweepings. The "stores" grossed $60,000 in less than two years. With the profits, Marguerite purchased a prime, half-acre city lot for just $750 and quickly leased it for $500 a month. But her biggest financial windfall was yet to come.

Not all of the Klondike women found financial success. After two years on the trail, Emily Craig and her husband arrived too late to cash in on the rush. While her husband left to chase dreams of gold in Nome, Alaska, Emily stayed on in Dawson for a few months as a cook. Then she reluctantly left to join him, "wishing [she] was back in Chicago and wondering why [she] came."

Years after her husband died, Emily remained in the North, employed as a hospital worker in Anchorage, Alaska. There she met and married Dr. J. H. Romig, and the couple later retired to Colorado.

Women of the Creeks

A veteran of a dozen mining camps, Nellie Cashman invested her restaurant returns in claims. She was soon beset with legal disputes. The most serious allegation was that Nellie had tried to bribe Belinda Mulrooney by threatening to reveal information about Belinda's business associations with the mining inspector. Commissioner William Ogilvie was forced to investigate, and Nellie confessed she had been in error.

Her obvious record of community work stood her in good stead, and no charges were laid.

Nellie struck it big with "19 below" (the first, or "discovery" claim) on Bonanza Creek. She eventually bought out her partners, while her crew carted away more than $100,000 of ore. The proceeds bought her less-profitable claims, which she travelled to on snowshoe or with her dog team.

Martha Purdy, now a single mother, managed to stake some claims with her brother on Excelsior Creek. Within a few months, the claims were worth tens of thousands of dollars, and Martha and her partners employed a crew of 16. It wasn't long before Martha's sawmill foreman decided that he "wasn't gonna be run by a skirt." He persuaded the entire crew to quit, and equipment was sabotaged. The foreman was the prime suspect. Unable to lay charges, the Mounties bluntly advised him to leave the Klondike.

For legal advice, Martha turned to fellow Klondiker, lawyer George Black. In the course of conversation, George mentioned that he was interested in becoming a politician. George also suggested he was interested in something else — marriage to Martha. It took Martha two years to accept his proposal, but when she did, her life changed forever. Decades later, the couple moved to Ottawa. George was now speaker of the House of Commons, and later, Martha became a member of parliament at age 69.

The Klondike Mogul
Within days of her party's arrival in the Klondike, feisty, Irish-born entrepreneur Belinda Mulrooney began to explore retail opportunities in Canada's newest northern settlement. She partnered with three newcomers from Circle City, Alaska: a woman of questionable virtue named Esther Duffie, and two married women who had braved the icy Yukon River.

Belinda had brought long, metal cylinders full of silks over the Chilkoot Trail.

"I've been a fool," she thought bitterly, fearing that no one would buy delicate silks in such a boom-town environment. Hiding her embarrassment, Belinda opened one of the cylinders. The others greedily fingered the silk garments, and Belinda's discomfort about how she would earn an income vanished.

Belinda watched prospectors' native wives shuffle down the waterfront pathway in mukluks, short skirts, and heavy work shirts. They came to the store, dashed away, and returned a while later, dragging their grizzled husbands.

Esther Duffie would hold up a particularly exquisite item for the couples to view.

"What's that good for?" one miner shouted.

"That'll be a fine outfit when the mosquitoes get after you," laughed another.

Many of the women did not know how to wear the items their men bought. They were happy enough to own such fine fashions and to feel the silk in their hands.

"Next!" Esther would holler. "Who wants a beautiful night dress?"

Clever and beguiling, Esther manipulated the scales weighing the prospectors' gold in a way that made even Belinda blush. Esther might have been merely a whore in Circle City, but she was a formidable saleswoman in Dawson. Belinda earned a 600 percent profit on the sale of her goods.

The women wanted silks; the men wanted meals. There was only one problem: a supply shortage. Belinda knew that every man with an outfit was a potential restaurant customer. She proposed an offer few men could refuse. If they gave her their food, they would receive either credit at her new restaurant, or cash. Most of the men hated cooking, so the restaurant's inventory swelled. In the land of the midnight sun, Belinda's restaurant did a roaring trade, 24 hours a day.

With the profits, Belinda bought lots on Front Street, which faced the Yukon River. She dismantled river rafts and turned them into money-making cabins. After visiting the creeks, Belinda developed an idea that had the miners rolling with mirth: she decided to build a hotel where the Eldorado angled away from the Bonanza. The laughing stopped when the newly finished, two-storey Grand Forks Hotel quickly filled with tenants. Before long, a town had sprung up all around the establishment. Belinda's dream, however, was to build a hotel in the heart of Dawson City. She would call the three-storey structure the Fairview.

Others, including prospector-millionaire Alex Mc-Donald — Belinda's rival and partner — shook their heads.

"Alex and … Joe Barrette don't want you to try and build that hotel," Grand Forks Hotel manager Walter Gilmer told Belinda. "They don't feel you can make a go of it."

"I guess that's just why I'm going to build it," Belinda answered defiantly. "If they didn't say that, I wouldn't think of it."

Belinda secretly arranged a $10,000 bet that she would finish the hotel. One bet became many. Men even bet she would never be able to heat the building. They hadn't counted on her innovative "central heating" system: a large coal-oil tank converted into a furnace. Later, she was told that men had put up as much as $100,000.

Build the hotel she did, and she won the bets, too. The hotel was "by far the most prestigious structure now in Dawson," raved the *Nugget*. From Grand Forks, some eight kilometres away, the mining inspector declared the hotel open, making his grand announcement via a new invention called the telephone. There were speeches, food, champagne, and dancing to the music of — as Belinda put it — "one perfectly equipped orchestra." It was a triumph for the mogul, who was all of 27 years old.

Belinda was more than a visionary. Regardless of the obstacles she faced, tenacious Belinda managed to turn dreams into realities, not only for her own profit, but for the betterment of Dawson. From hotels and sanitary water systems to telephone and fire services, Belinda Mulrooney's energy, influence, and cash were behind them all.

The pressure had been relentless throughout the hotel's construction. Belinda had needed building supplies. Once again, time was the enemy. In Skagway, she told packer Joe Brooks it was imperative that he deliver supplies from the port city to Lake Bennett in just three days. He agreed, and charged her premium fees for the task. Belinda concluded that if Joe could manage the delivery, it was worth the high price. She raced to Bennett to await the supplies. An employee hurried after Belinda, telling her that Joe Brooks had dumped her supplies at the summit of the pass! Saloon keeper Bill McPhee had offered the packer more money to move his whiskey to the Bennett steamboats. Belinda was enraged.

Belinda and her employee rode up to the summit, hired a bunch of tough men on the trail, and rode down past the North-West Mounted Police post into U.S. territory. There they could ambush Joe and his boys without running afoul of Canadian law. As Joe's mule train ambled up, loaded with Bill McPhee's supplies, Belinda trotted into the centre of the trail. She calmly told the foreman she wouldn't budge until he had read one specific clause of her contract with Joe Brooks. The clause stated she could take possession of Joe's pack-train mules at any time if the conditions of the contract were not met.

"We're not bothered with a contract, woman," the foreman snarled. It seemed like a stand-off, but Belinda was prepared. She had every intention of enforcing the clause.

"Well, you'll have a hell of a chance taking *this* pack train," the foreman laughed.

"Well, old man," Belinda smiled, urging her horse up to the foreman's, "I hate to do it, but I must." Suddenly the foreman blanched and looked down at the barrel of Belinda's revolver, which was prodding him painfully beneath his belt. "You better get off," Belinda warned. The foreman dismounted.

Actually, Belinda felt she was doing the fellow a favour. "I only pulled the gun on him to give him a decent excuse for giving up the mules," she confessed. "A man had to have a decent excuse in Skagway. Of course, my men took the foreman and messed him up enough to make him feel it was a real holdup."

Belinda's gang took the mules, unloaded Bill McPhee's liquor, loaded up her supplies, and took the foreman in tow. Then she offered Joe Brooks's men jobs, which they eagerly accepted.

"Brooks's crew thought it was all a wonderful joke on him," Belinda recalled. To inflame their former boss even further, the men gave Belinda Joe's horse.

"Everyone on the trail knew Brooks's pinto," Belinda laughed later. "Said I might as well have it. That horse was the swellest little animal I ever knew."

Years went by, and Miss Belinda Mulrooney became Mrs. Charles Carbonneau, the wife of a supposed French count (or perhaps a Montreal barber — nobody knows for sure). As the couple's wealth increased and their mine holdings grew, the two spent winters in Paris and summers in the Klondike, and later, in Fairbanks, Alaska, where she founded a bank. By 1906, Belinda was divorced (she called herself a widow), and she retired to Carbonneau Castle in Yakima, Washington. In the late 1920s, she rented the castle for extra income. In 1943, the 71-year-old former Klondike mogul donned a hard hat to help build mine sweepers for the Associated Ship Builders.

"Well, why not?" she told an interviewer in her typical, no-nonsense style. "I've really worked all my life and this is certainly no time to be idle. We've got a war to win."

Chapter 9
Citizens of the Demimonde

Laundry, cooking, accommodation, and hot baths weren't the only services women made available to thousands of Klondike gold seekers. For many men, especially those who had been successful on the creeks, "hospitality" services were priority purchases.

Practitioners of "the oldest profession," "citizens of the demimonde," "soiled doves," and "ladies of the tenderloin" were some of the euphemisms polite society (and its sniggering newspaper writers) used to describe the women who worked as prostitutes. They were part of the Yukon culture long before George Carmack and his partners made their enormous strike.

Dancing Across the Line of Decorum

In her biography, Martha (Purdy) Black maintained there were three classes of women in the Klondike: those of "the oldest profession," dance-hall and variety girls, and a few others, including "wives of an unbounded faith in and love for their mate." Martha grouped entertainers with prostitutes and in doing so, reflected the prevailing attitude of the day. In some instances, she may have been correct in her assumption. Nobody knows how many dance-hall and variety girls strayed across the line of morality as circumstances — or perhaps, opportunities — dictated. However, as Belinda Mulrooney insisted, some women actually stepped the other way.

"Many who got caught in the mess of the trail changed their names and when they got to Dawson, started to swing men around in the dance hall. Some never took a drink. Maybe you don't know it," Belinda told an interviewer, "but some of the best women in the northwest today have been in those Klondike dance halls."

Dance-hall girls were not, despite popular belief, chorus-line women who did high kicks on stages. Instead, they were the women paid by lonely men to simply dance with them, working the floor between shows, shuffling through more than 100 dances a night. They were also called "percentage girls," because they received a commission on the dollar-a-dance money they earned on the floor or in the theatre boxes, where, as "box-rushers," they enticed men to drink away their rawhide pokes of gold dust.

Ladies of the evening "at work." Behind the group are the notorious "cribs," each with enough room for a bed, a chair, and a washstand.

Often entertainers stepped back and forth over the invisible line between legitimate work and prostitution. Many entertainers and dance-hall girls made more than $200 a month, much more than Sam Steele's police constables took back to their barracks, and even more than many hard-working prospectors managed to wrench out of the ground. A few, such as Mae Field and New York stage actress Esther Lyon (alias Cad Wilson), were well received in theatres, saloons, and dance halls, as well as in the parlours of polite society. When Cad Wilson left the Yukon in the summer of 1899, she packed up $26,000 and a huge nugget necklace.

Mae Field turned to prostitution out of pure desperation.

Arriving in the Klondike as newlyweds in 1898, Mae and Arthur Field managed to accomplish what others only dreamed of doing: they made a $100,000 gold strike. However, lady luck turned fickle. Arthur invested badly, lost everything, and abandoned his wife. Fortunately, Mae soon made an exciting discovery of her own: she possessed genuine theatrical talent. The Flora Dora Dance Hall operators agreed, and before long, as "The Doll Of Dawson," Mae was one of the city's most popular performers.

Mae was not alone in fending off starvation through prostitution. A young Seattle woman whom the *Klondike Nugget* dubbed "Milley Lane" also took up the oldest profession.

"That is not her name; we cannot advertise these people," the newspaper sniffed, ignoring the more compassionate reason for the phoney pseudonym; namely, protecting the true identity of the unfortunate woman. Destitute and hungry after three fruitless days of job hunting, Milley had but two choices, according to the newspaper: "jump into the river or go to board with one of the madams in Dawson's Whitechapel." Whitechapel was the newspaper's ill-conceived attempt at a parallel with the notorious lowlife district of London, England. Milley's trail acquaintances, who hadn't given the woman a hand up or even a handout, professed shock that she chose "the madams."

As Belinda Mulrooney's long-time employee, Esther Duffie was more fortunate than most. Belinda proved to be a broad-minded, practical employer. After the Front Street tent store folded, Esther found work in Belinda's restaurant, and was later one of the kitchen crew at the Fairview Hotel's grand opening celebration. A few weeks later, more to appease the righteous than for any other reason, the North-West Mounted Police staged a rare, well-publicized tenderloin raid. They rounded up 69 of the soiled doves, including Esther Duffie. Belinda, who "never lost respect and liking" for Esther, offered forgiveness, choosing to ignore her friend's carousing lifestyle, saying, "both my eyes were shut when she went on a spree."

Along with her friend Belinda, Esther eventually journeyed to Alaska to be part of the gold rush excitement in Fairbanks.

Like all other Klondikers, prostitutes came from around the globe, from as far away as Sweden, Germany, France, and Japan. Martha (Purdy) Black recalled a group from Belgium that arrived in 1898. The women offered their services in Dawson City, Lousetown, and Grand Forks.

Wherever they worked, most prostitutes lived in poverty. When a prospector walked out of the crib, he usually left behind a few ounces of gold dust. There was little of it left for the women to spend after their pimps or madams came to collect. The Klondike's high prices quickly emptied their purses of what remained. During freeze-up, claim holders could not wash gold from the creeks, and their incomes suffered. In preparation for pending hardships, Mabel Larose auctioned herself off for the winter in the Monte Carlo Saloon. When the bidding was done, Mabel had fetched room, board, and $5,000 in exchange for her exclusive services. She was likely the envy of many of her colleagues.

Life and Death on the Wrong Side of Town

Life was difficult for almost everyone during the gold rush, but women living in Dawson's tenderloin districts faced unthinkable risks.

As bystanders in a Dawson City alley carried a gunshot victim, Mrs. La Ghrist, to the Good Samaritan Hospital, the North-West Mounted Police elbowed their way into her shack. Having squeezed through the blocked entrance, they discovered the woman's husband, John La Ghrist, lying jammed between the door and a wall, a bullet hole in his temple.

The La Ghrist shooting was Dawson City's third sordid murder-suicide during the three gold-rush years. The first two women died with their murderous men. John La Ghrist was less successful than his predecessors. Despite receiving three gunshot wounds, his estranged wife survived.

Anna DeGraf, a gifted seamstress, worked closely with prostitutes and their abusers in Juneau, Circle City, and Dawson City. She knew the dangers faced by gold rush women and Anna assisted the "women of the mean streets" beyond simply sewing their gowns. Anna quickly earned a reputation as a feisty, no-nonsense woman after she smashed a would-be thief across the face with a log from her fireside woodpile.

One night, a dance-hall girl burst into Anna's home, begging for help. Six men had broken into the dancer's cabin and had attempted to rape her. In fighting off her attackers, the woman had been burned badly on the surface of her stove. A few minutes later, the men surrounded Anna's cabin and demanded she release their victim. Anna refused. They began beating down her door. Anna pulled out the six-gun she had been given by her employer, the Alaska Commercial company manager, and fired three shots through the cabin door. The would-be assailants ran for cover.

During the time she later lived and worked in Dawson, Anna delivered matching blue dresses to a pair of dancers. Upon Anna's arrival at the women's hotel room, one of the dancers immediately burst into tears. She led Anna to her room mate, who lay dead on floor, the result of an apparent lover's suicide. The woman's husband had cheated on her, causing her such sadness that she took her own life. Curious about the commotion, her husband entered the hotel room, stood in the doorway, lit a cigarette, then calmly walked away from the mess. The dress was given to another dancer, and the show continued as scheduled.

Making the Most of It All

Not all prostitutes and dance-hall girls were innocent, big-hearted victims. Some of them were paid to take advantage of the men they enticed. These talents came naturally to women who schemed beyond professional fleecing in saloons and dance halls.

Juneau's "Queen of Burlesque," 20-year-old Violet Raymond, arrived in Dawson City when tents still lined the river bank. She and others in an entertainment troupe opened the log-built two-storey Opera House. Violet's Klondike career lasted just four weeks. During that time, she met and charmed Clarence Berry's partner, Anton Stander, one of the wealthiest Eldorado Creek claim owners. When Violet and Anton left the Yukon, $75,000 of the prospector's $200,000 haul was already in Violet's name. Anton's jealous, drunken rages soon sent the former entertainer packing. Anton died a pauper, as much a victim of alcohol and worthless future mining as he was of Violet Raymond's avarice. However, when Violet passed away in 1944, her estate was worth $50,000, a sizeable fortune in the days when the average annual salary was less than $1,200.

Nineteen-year-old Gussie Lamore enchanted diminutive "Swiftwater" Bill Gates, another wealthy claim holder who left a large poke of gold dust lying at her feet and a marriage proposal ringing in her ears. She accepted his invitation and swindled him out of a small fortune before blithely stepping onto a steamer bound for San Francisco.

"He was too easy — the easiest thing you ever saw," she confessed to the *Seattle Daily Times*. "All you had to do was touch him for $500 and get it. But I wouldn't have married him for all the gold in the Klondike."

Monte Carlo entertainer Grace Drummond left her husband, Edgar Mizner, after the pompous merchant lost nearly $20,000 in one night of reckless roulette play. Grace promised to move in with another Klondike millionaire, Charlie "Lucky Swede" Anderson, if he would put $50,000 in her bank account. Charlie, who had drunkenly purchased what became one of the Klondike's richest claims, quickly agreed. The happy couple toured Europe before returning to San Francisco, where they built a mansion and invested in real estate. Unfortunately, the San Francisco earthquake levelled their investments. Before long, Grace and the fortune were gone, and Charlie spent his last years working as a labourer in a British Columbia sawmill.

Dawson cigar store operator Marguerite Laimee reaped the rewards of the Klondike's biggest matrimonial pay off. The "businesswoman" was a guest at a lavish dinner at one of the city's hotels when she noticed a good-looking gent across the room. Marguerite had not recognized his face, but she certainly recognized his name: George Carmack, the man whose Bonanza Creek strike had started the world's greatest gold rush.

Marguerite's timing was perfect. George had just returned from the outside, beset with professional and personal problems. Attractive, 26-year-old Marguerite so bedazzled the troubled man that he asked her to marry him before the night was done. Marguerite didn't hesitate to accept. She promised to sell her Dawson properties and settle with him in Seattle. Less than two weeks later, George and Marguerite boarded a train to Skagway, never to return to the North.

For many years, life was good for the Carmacks. Real estate properties brought them many riches. After George died of pneumonia, his daughter and sister sued Marguerite for the estate. When the dust settled and the legal wrangling was over, Marguerite was still a wealthy woman. However, mining prospects she had purchased with the remains of George's Klondike fortune proved worthless. When she died in 1942, Marguerite lived in a modest house, having lost millions of dollars.

Of all the entertainers, dance-hall girls, and prostitutes, only one enjoyed long-lasting notoriety in the decades that followed. Even though Kate Rockwell arrived in Dawson at the end of the rush, over time she came to personify the Klondike's heyday.

Kate managed to wring more public relations value out of her two brief years in the Yukon than any other person. She enjoyed appearances in Hollywood, in the press, on radio, and even on television. Single-handedly, Kate kept the rags-to-riches lure of the Klondike alive, and would eventually manage to turn tragedy into a personal triumph.

From all accounts, Kate's dance-hall performances were spectacular, and she became a Dawson City sensation. However, for the woman who inscribed her photos, "Mush on and smile," it was as much her warm personality as her

Unlike many Dawson dance-hall girls and prostitutes, Kate "Kitty" Rockwell possessed a timeless, classical beauty that captivated thousands of men.

performances that won the hearts of thousands of men. One day in 1900, she noticed a handsome, swarthy waiter working at the Savoy. The waiter's name was Alexander Pantages.

Ambitious and creative, Alexander envisioned owning a chain of theatres, and before long, Kate became part of his plan. Kate's talent had already guaranteed her own wealth. Based on Alexander's promise of marriage, Kate began to bankroll the now-jobless waiter's first venture, the Orpheum Theatre. Later, in Seattle, as the theatre chain began to take shape, Alexander married someone else. Kate's 1905 breach of promise suit brought her less than $5,000.

From time to time, Kate tapped Alexander for money, and the nervous millionaire paid, fearful that this still-lovely ghost from his past might injure his reputation. In 1929, a 17-year-old dancer charged the theatre mogul with assault and rape. Kate, the self-styled "Queen of the Yukon," received a subpoena from the district attorney's office. Her world was never the same again.

When the guilty verdict was read, Kate's heart-breaking story was splashed over the front page of the Los Angeles *Evening Herald.* Photographs showed her clenching a handkerchief, dabbing at nonexistent tears. Kate received amazing media coverage, considering she never took the stand.

"I never testified against Alexander Pantages," she said, taking full credit for her absence of testimony, "because win or lose, a sourdough never squeals."

The notoriety had made her both a celebrity and a legend. Two years later, Kate married Johnny Matson, a real-life sourdough who had fallen in love with her after seeing her perform in Dawson City some 30 years earlier. The old prospector was still wandering the Yukon, looking for the mother lode. Their Vancouver wedding made international news. Kate became the subject of numerous interviews. She took a turn as parade marshal, participated in ribbon cuttings, and finally, she received an on-screen credit as Hollywood technical advisor to the producers of her celluloid life story.

"Entirely fictional," she sniffed. In hotel lobbies and high-class restaurants, she would hike up her skirt to show off her still-shapely legs, and demonstrate how she "rolled her own" for a really satisfying sourdough smoke.

"If I had my life to live over, I wouldn't do it much differently," she said proudly. "I've done a lot of living since the days when I was a girl with flaming red hair and twinkling feet. I've had fame and fortune, joy and heartbreak, but I wouldn't change a minute of it."

Others felt much the same way. Over time, the trials and tribulations so many women suffered seemed somehow trivial. Contentment and satisfaction came from the wild, untamed land as much as anything else.

"It takes the solitude of frozen nights with the howl of dogs for company, the glistening fairness of days when nature reaches out and loves you, she's so beautiful, to bring out the soul in folks," Nellie Cashman maintained. "Banging trolley cars, honking cars, clubs for catty women and false standards of living won't do it."

"You just feast on it," Belinda Mulrooney said of the Yukon. "You become quite religious, seem to get inspiration. Or it might be the electricity in the air. You are filled with it, ready to go."

"I could not shake off the lure of the Klondike," Martha (Purdy) Black admitted, recalling how unhappy she had been while visiting her parents in Kansas for a brief period in 1899. "My thoughts were continually of that vast new, rugged country, its stark and splendid mountains, its lordly Yukon River."

Unknowingly speaking for the hundreds of women who left their world behind, Martha added, "What I wanted was not shelter and safety, but liberty and opportunity."

Acknowledgments

This author owes a debt of gratitude to many writers whose works helped make this book possible. Chief among them is author and professor emerita of the University of California, Melanie J. Mayer. Mayer's *Klondike Women* does much to shed light on the life and times of the "fairer sex" in the Klondike. Her exhaustive biography of Belinda Mulrooney, *Staking Her Claim*, co-authored with noted Alaska historian, Robert DeArmond, provides much more than a comprehensive account of one of the wealthiest women in the Klondike. In telling Belinda's story, the scholarly work provides many fascinating glimpses of Dawson City, Grand Forks, and the people who inhabited the Klondike during the gold rush.

Four Canadian books — including an autobiography of a Klondike pioneer — provided invaluable material for this volume. Martha Louise Black's *My Ninety Years* is among the best eye-witness accounts of the Klondike Gold Rush era. In telling Kate Ryan's story, T. Ann Brennan's *The Real Klondike Kate* provided a much-needed account of travels on the Stikine Trail. Two comprehensive overviews, Francis Backhouse's *Women of the Klondike* and Jennifer Duncan's more recent *Frontier Spirit* provided a wealth of detail on the experiences of many "rebel women" of the Klondike.

Sadly, very few actual first-hand accounts of the dance-hall girls, entertainers, and prostitutes were documented.

Even fewer of these writings survive today. It is fortunate that copies of Dawson City's first and best-known newspaper, *The Klondike Nugget*, still exist. Stories from its pages tell us much about the Klondike's "Paradise Alley." Many of these reports are gathered together in Jay Moynahan's *Red Light Revelations*. Tales of the habitués of the "wrong side of town" are also related in one of the first of the post–World War II books to attempt to tell the gold rush story, *High Jinks on the Klondike*, by Richard O'Connor.

Bibliography

Backhouse, Francis. *Women of the Klondike*. Vancouver: Whitecap Books, 2002.

Berton, Pierre. *Klondike, The Last Great Gold Rush*. Toronto: McClelland & Stewart Ltd., rev. ed., 1975.

Black, Martha Louise. *My Ninety Years*. Anchorage, Alaska: Northwest Publishing Company, 1976.

Brennan, Ann T. *The Real Klondike Kate*. Fredericton: Goose Lane Editions, 1990.

Bronson, William. *The Last Grand Adventure*. New York: McGraw-Hill Book Company, 1977.

Duncan, Jennifer. *Frontier Spirit: The Brave Women Of The*

Yukon. Toronto: Anchor Canada, a Division of Random House of Canada Limited, 2004.

Johnson, James Albert. *George Carmack.* Vancouver: Whitecap Books, 2001.

Lucia, Ellis. *Klondike Kate.* New York: Hastings House Publishers, 1962.

Mayer, Melanie J. *Klondike Women.* Athens, Ohio: Swallow Press, 1989.

Mayer, Melanie J. and Robert N. DeArmond. *Staking Her Claim: The Life of Belinda Mulrooney.* Athens, Ohio: Swallow Press, 2000.

Moynahan, Jay. *Red Light Revelations.* Spokane, Washington: Chickadee Publishing, 2001.

Murphy, Claire Rudolf and Haigh, Jane G. *Gold Rush Women.* Anchorage, Alaska: Northwest Books, 1997.

O'Connor, Richard. *High Jinks on the Klondike.* New York: Bobbs-Merrill Company, Ltd., 1954.

Porsild, Charlene. *Gamblers and Dreamers.* Vancouver: UBC Press, 1998.

Steele, Samuel B. *Forty Years in Canada.* Toronto: McGraw-Hill Ryerson Ltd., 1972.

Walden, Arthur T. *A Dog Puncher On The Yukon.* Cambridge, Massachusetts: Houghton Mifflin Company, 1928.

About the Author

One of Altitude Publishing's most prolific authors, Rich Mole has enjoyed an eclectic communications career as broadcaster, freelance journalist, corporate consultant, and for 20 years, as the president of a successful Vancouver Island advertising agency.

Rich is the author of several other Amazing Stories: *Christmas in BC, Christmas in the Prairies, Edmonton Oilers, Gold Fever,* and *Great Stanley Cup Victories.*

Rich Mole makes his home in Calgary, Alberta, and can be reached at ramole@telus.net.

Photo Credits

Cover: Yukon Archives, MacBride Museum collection (3795); Alaska State Library: page 59 (Winter and Pond photographers, PCA-87-682); Dawson City Museum: page 121 (984-98-4); Glenbow Archives: page 72 (NA-891-5); National Archives of Canada (Ottawa): page 113 (C-014478); Yukon Archives: pages 85, 91 (M. L. Black Collection, 82/218, H-14).